CONTENTS

Foreword — vii

Introduction — ix

STEP ONE: Celebrate — 1

STEP TWO: Protect — 11

STEP THREE: Nourish — 26

STEP FOUR: Love — 54

STEP FIVE: Inspire — 65

STEP SIX: Challenge — 74

STEP SEVEN: Connect — 87

STEP EIGHT: Define — 97

STEP NINE: Detach — 105

STEP TEN: Praise — 115

STEP ELEVEN: Laugh — 124

STEP TWELVE: Listen — 132

STEP THIRTEEN: Release — 142

STEP FOURTEEN: Prioritise — 152

but perhaps this one was a big one because she had come of age. I, in the true manner of all mistrusting little kids, furrowed my brow furiously. I ended up feeling rather sorry for the poor princess who, in my head, had never had a birthday party ever until she was sixteen. At that moment, I was one up on a princess, because I'd had a birthday party for all my eight years.

As I grew, I realised that the parties were not the only way my parents celebrated me. And it is only now, that I am a parent myself that I realise how I need to learn from what they did. I realised we think so far into the future that we constantly tend to forget the here and now, and that is the place children live in: the present. Every moment we have with them is a celebration of sorts. As Antoine de Saint-Exupéry said in *The Little Prince,* 'All grown-ups were once children ... but only few of them remember it.'

The offspring came eight years after our marriage. We had sown all our wild oats, and were so ready to be responsible, calm, mature parents. But the first time I held my son, a bomb of panic exploded in my chest. I was now responsible for this delicate life. Honestly, I felt kind of shortchanged. This little creature looked nothing remotely cute and baby-like at that moment, freshly out of the womb. Squished up face, red like a tomato, still slimy from the blood post C-Sec. Where was the myth of the fresh smelling, gurgling, baby powder smelling bundle of cuteness the television ads had sold me? He opened his eyes, stared at me for one long second. I was the first thing he saw in his life, I realised. I hoped it enhanced his fledgling view of the world he'd

STEP ONE: CELEBRATE

Celebrate in little ways, every single day. Because your child is your own personal little miracle.

There's a fairy story I remember from my childhood. It was a story of a princess. Her father, the king, celebrated her sixteenth birthday with great pomp and splendour, inviting the entire kingdom and all the neighbouring kingdoms to the festivities. Psst, in retrospect, it was probably the king's way of putting the flag out that the princess was now eligible for marriage but at that point I had no clue of this phenomenon of announcing a girl's coming of marriageable age.

To my then innocent mind, the fact that there was absolutely no mention about the celebrating of her previous birthdays had outraged me and I was up in arms on behalf of the princess. 'Was this her first birthday party?' I asked my father, who was reading out the story to me. 'Didn't they celebrate any other birthday for her?'

My father, God bless his soul, did his best to reassure me that of course, they had celebrated all previous birthdays,

But Ashwin convinced me that indeed, this was a book that needed to be written and that he would, indeed, co-write it. So gathering the above-mentioned skittering nerves, I set about trying to figure out one could indeed distil down the wisdom of what good, nay, bloody good parenting comprised of, into 13 steps. So this book isn't me clambered onto a pedestal and dispensing parenting gyaan. Far from it. It is advice from around the world that I could have and still can use in my parenting journey, and that I hope will be useful to anyone trying to raise a child to the best of their ability. With personal anecdotes from my own experiences of child-rearing and from friends around me, examples from history, a fair amount of conclusions from research conducted around the globe and time-tested wisdom handed down over the generations, *13 Steps to Bloody Good Parenting* takes you through the most important things you need to focus on in your parenting journey, which surprisingly, are the simplest things you could ever do.

And, of course, as Alvin Toffler wisely said, 'Parenthood remains the greatest single preserve of the amateur.' Nonetheless, as amateurs, we do stumble through parenthood, giving our best to the most demanding job in our lives.

Kiran Manral
Mumbai, 2018

did the best I could with the little bundle of life entrusted to me, and am still struggling. The arsenal of advice from well-meaning friends and family around me, some common sense, a trustworthy paediatrician, the convenience of Google baba, and the mantra of 'this too shall pass', got me through the early years. Over the years, I have been reading voraciously on the topic of parenting, seeing how parenting styles have evolved from the time I was a child, and how my mom's model of 'because I said so', just didn't work anymore. I wrote a blog about my experiences in bringing up my son—good, bad and ugly—and the blog went on to be rather popular, and eventually made its way into a book. This was all, of course, anecdotal. But actual tips as in telling good folks how to parent, I quivered in my size six shoes at the presumptuousness of doing so. I should've taken heed from the wise Dr Benjamin Spock though, when he said, 'Trust yourself. You know more than you think you do.' In that sense, this book has been a learning experience for me, too. The things I did. The things I didn't. What I must adopt immediately, and why it's never too late to incorporate something into one's parenting style.

Time for a little confession here. Ashwin has been a rock of encouragement and support, at times in my writing career when I was most down and out, and I owe him the courage I found to get out of a 'I'm not cut out to be a writer' funk. When the idea of this book came up, I found my nerves skittering around like a ball of yarn that had fallen with a thud onto the floor. 'I'm the last person to be giving parenting advice,' I protested. 'My offspring is proof!'

in therapy, listing out all the times I've inadvertently warped him for life. I hope, though, that he remembers that I ruined my bones, my figure and developed stretch marks because of him, and keeps that in mind when he's picking out my old-age home.

It is a tough job being a parent. It is also the world's most easily available job. One doesn't need to train for it. One needs no qualifications for it. Yet, one is a parent, often by choice, sometimes by chance, but always, especially the first time round, completely unprepared.

In this hyper-informative age, parenting is much like tap dancing in a minefield. While most parents have nothing to draw from except their experience with their own parents, most are now confronted by a battalion of information and advice from a slew of parenting experts. Most of these opinions are so conflicting that they would make for dinner guests who don't speak with each other in a civil manner.

To add to our confusion, there are all the labels that have been plastered onto parenting. Democratic parenting, helicopter parenting, laissez-faire parenting, tiger mom parenting, autocratic parenting, neglectful parenting, permissive parenting, French parenting, and of course, my school of parenting which is the 'I hope I'm getting this right' parenting. As Billy Graham, the evangelist, stated wisely, 'Parenting is the most important responsibility most of us will ever face, and none of us does it perfectly.'

We can never be perfect parents, because there are no perfect parents. Like everyone, I too, hit the ground running and

INTRODUCTION

It is always with great trepidation that I write about parenting. The only thing that qualifies me to put down anything on the subject is the fact that I produced from my womb, a single squalling offspring, red-faced and very irate at being removed from the comfortable spot he was in. And I've managed, in the past fourteen years, to get through the years with my sanity intact. The comedian, Jerry Seinfeld, joked that having a two-year old is like owning a blender without the top. I now realise why.

I haven't been a perfect parent. Far from it. And the offspring is not the poster boy for anything that would qualify me to write this book. To be honest, he's not the poster boy for anything except insolence, now that he's entered his teens.

In that I'm not alone. The human race has survived because we've reproduced and created offspring, never mind the times I've wished I had tied my tubes given how surly the newly-minted teen has become. But then, few of us could lay claim to the title of being perfect parents, our own included. Parenting is a topic fraught with so much responsibility that I quiver when I think of my son, many years down the line,

13 STEPS TO BLOODY GOOD PARENTING

Ashwin Sanghi is counted among India's highest selling English authors. He has written several bestsellers (*The Rozabal Line, Chanakya's Chant, The Krishna Key, The Sialkot Saga, Keepers of the Kalachakra, The Vault of Vishnu,* and *The Magicians of Mazda* in his *Bharat Series*) and two *New York Times* bestselling crime thrillers with James Patterson, *Private India* (sold in the US as *City on Fire*) and *Private Delhi* (sold in the US as *Count to Ten*). Ashwin also mentors, co-writes and edits titles in this popular *13 Steps Series* on subjects as diverse as Luck, Wealth, Marks, Health and Parenting.

He is a regular contributor to the Op-Ed pages of the *Times of India*. Ashwin has been included by *Forbes India* in their Celebrity 100 and by the *New Indian Express* in their Culture Power List. He is a winner of the Crossword Popular Choice Award 2012, Atta Galatta Popular Choice Award 2018, WBR Iconic Achievers Award 2018, the Lit-O-Fest Literature Legend Award 2018, the Kalinga Popular Choice Award 2021 and the Deendayal Upadhyaya Recognition 2023. He was educated at Cathedral and John Connon School, Mumbai, and St Xavier's College, Mumbai. He holds a Master's from Yale University, USA, and a D. Litt. (Honoris Causa) from JECRC University, Rajasthan. Ashwin lives in Mumbai with his wife, Anushika, and his son, Raghuvir.

Website: www.sanghi.in
Facebook: www.facebook.com/ashwinsanghi
Twitter: www.twitter.com/ashwinsanghi
YouTube: www.youtube.com/ashwinsanghi
Instagram: instagram.com/ashwin.sanghi
LinkedIn: www.linkedin.com/in/ashwinsanghi

FOREWORD

When I wrote *13 Steps to Bloody Good Luck* in 2014, I had imagined it as a single one-off book, certainly not the beginning of a series. But that changed when readers' comments began coming in. They wondered why other subjects could not be demystified as well. Thus, the book that you hold in your hands follows three previous titles: *13 Steps to Bloody Good Luck*, *13 Steps to Bloody Good Wealth*, and *13 Steps to Bloody Good Marks*. As I write this foreword, two more titles, *13 Steps to Bloody Good Health* and *13 Steps to Bloody Good Sales* are also in the works.

The political satirist P.J. O'Rourke once observed, 'Everybody knows how to raise children, except the people who have them.' And while those words were uttered in jest, there is something that rings true about them. No child arrives with an instruction manual or warranty booklet. Parents are saddled with the frightening job of navigating their way through unfamiliar territory. For the most part, they're driving blind.

I have an admission to make: I know very little about good parenting. My fifteen-year old son, Raghuvir, can vouch for

First published by Westland Publications Private Limited in 2019

Published by Westland Books, a division of Nasadiya Technologies Private Limited in 2023

No. 269/2B, First Floor, 'Irai Arul', Vimalraj Street, Nethaji Nagar, Alapakkam Main Road, Maduravoyal, Chennai 600095

Westland and the Westland logo are the trademarks of Nasadiya Technologies Private Limited, or its affiliates.

Copyright © Ashwin Sanghi, 2019

Ashwin Sanghi asserts the moral right to be identified as the author of this work.

ISBN: 9789395767781

10 9 8 7 6 5 4 3 2 1

The views and opinions expressed in this work are the author's own and the facts are as reported by him, and the publisher is in no way liable for the same.

All rights reserved

Typeset in Arno Pro by SÜRYA, New Delhi
Printed at Nutech Print Services-India

No part of this book may be reproduced, or stored in a retrieval system, or transmitted in any form or by any means, electronic, mechanical, photocopying, recording, or otherwise, without express written permission of the publisher.

13 STEPS TO BLOODY GOOD PARENTING

ASHWIN SANGHI
KIRAN MANRAL

emerged in, but I would never know, of course. I realised the truth of what Roald Dahl said in *Matilda* right then, 'It's a funny thing about mothers and fathers. Even when their own child is the most disgusting little blister you could ever imagine, they still think that he or she is wonderful.' I fell completely in love with him. The spouse, sadly, was relegated firmly to second spot at that moment.

Everything was a celebration in that first year of his babyhood: the first time he managed to flip himself onto his stomach, his first word, first tooth, first step, his first trip out of town, and never mind the nervous breakdown I almost had in the process. Slowly, the firsts began to be celebrated a little less. Like all relationships, I began to take my little miracle for granted. And so my world went on. Celebrations had been reduced to the annual event of the grand birthday party, with the balloons, the huge cake, the music and the return gifts, not to mention the ensuing two days one needed to recover from the exhaustion of organising it all. The miracle of my child kept unfolding in front of me every single day but I was taking note of it only once a year.

The other day, I realised he was no longer a child; he is now a teenager, and in a few years he would be grown up. And apart from the birthdays, there was little celebration we had done of the everyday. There was always something to get out of the way—potty training, school admissions, term examinations, final examinations, the list never ended. Celebrating one's child in the everyday sadly got relegated to the list of good intentions.

Why does a child need celebrating?

We don't realise it but children like to feel special, wanted and cherished. There's a fine balance to this of course. Too much of this and you could attach a basket to the ensuing helium head the child will develop and float skywards. Too little and the child might feel he or she isn't valued enough by their parents, and then grow up needing therapy to resolve abandonment issues.

How does one celebrate a child each day?

Is celebration the throwing of grand parties with games host, DJ, cake and hapless folks shovelled into cartoon character costumes? Not really, though those are good once a year. In the everyday, celebrating a child is anything from a dessert they're fond of to a day spent picnicking as a family.

Celebrating a child everyday might seem rather difficult on days when they're throwing the grandparent of all tantrums and making you seriously consider putting them up for adoption with the papers signed in triplicate (I kid, of course), but simply celebrating the moment and making it special could help create a bedrock of self-esteem to carry the child through the hormonal rollercoaster of adolescence and early adulthood. To pay heed to the ever so wise Erma Bombeck, 'Children make your life important.' How would they know how important they are to us unless we show them that they are?

I was at a leisurely luncheon the other day, with a group of friends, some of whom were mothers. I asked them how they celebrated their children. For a moment there was silence. The sangrias were downed a tad quicker while they pondered. Then answers began flowing in, and they weren't exactly what I thought they would be, but they were all food for thought.

'I bake a cake every time she scores well in her class tests.'

'We make sure we have one meal a day together as a family.'

'We get all her interesting art work framed and hung on a wall at the entrance of our home.'

'When he does a task on his own, he gets to choose what we all eat for dessert that night at dinner.'

'My daughter recently began dressing herself up on her own, and in celebration we took her out to a theme park for a day.'

'We have a wall of fame in the family, which is actually just a soft board decorated with tinsel and fairy lights, where every achievement no matter how little, gets posted.'

When all the responses had come in, and been tabulated in my mind, what remained was the realisation that they were all so different, but unified with the underlying premise that the celebrations didn't involve material things at all, but instead involved time, love and attention. These little gestures, I realised, were in the words of Swindell, '… deposits in the memory banks of our children.'

Here's how you could celebrate every day with your kids. And yes, there's always room for cake in any celebration, birthday or not. After all as Julia Child said, and any kid worth his sugar high would agree, 'A party without a cake is just a meeting.'

Don't miss the small moments

While a birthday is definitely a reason to celebrate, but so is a first fallen tooth. Going up a belt level in karate deserves a gift for sure, but learning to tie one's shoelaces and moving up from Velcro is also celebration worthy. It might deserve a hug, a kiss and a warm, heartfelt declaration of how proud you are she's learnt it. And perhaps an ice cream sundae or an unscheduled trip to the play zone. 'To be in your children's memories tomorrow, you have to be in their lives today,' observed the literary critic Barbara Johnson.

Eat dinner together

Every meal eaten together as a family is a mini-celebration of sorts, in this, an age where everyone is rushed off their feet and hard-pressed for time enough to sit down and eat together. Why is eating one meal together a celebration? It just affirms that family is important, and spending time with your kids is important to you as parents. Interestingly, eating dinner as a family has other benefits as well that you might not realise.

A 2010 study conducted by Elgar, Wendy Craig and Stephen Trites from Queen's University Canada reported that frequent family dinners together related to children having fewer emotional and behavioural problems. Family dinners, said the researchers, were chances for interactions between parents and children. This in turn had an impact on decisions involving nutrition, sharing of concerns and made the child feel cherished and loved. An additional benefit? Eating a meal regularly as a family gets the kids more eager to try out new foods and experiment with flavours if everyone is eating it.

Create bonding opportunities on a regular basis

When I was a child, my father would take me every Sunday morning to the beach, where I was allowed to swim in the water for the longest while. After this, I was given an ice-cream cone, heaped to tipping point with scoops of all the flavours available. The ice cream would inevitably melt as I struggled to finish it quickly, and my clothes would be a mess of stickiness as I wiped my hands on them to rid them of the melted ice cream. I realise now, in retrospect, that this was a great strategy to get me out of my mom's hair for a few hours on a Sunday, so she could spend time doing stuff she wanted to do.

These mornings at the beach slowly became a weekly ritual, one I would always inextricably associate with my father, and the beach became to me, a place of celebration of my childhood. Till today, I cannot pass Juhu beach in Mumbai without thinking of my father and the fun times we had in the sea and playing with the sand.

This was our 'bonding time', before the term 'bonding time' became popular in the parenting lexicon.

It doesn't have to be something lavish or expensive, or planned to the hilt. It could just be something as simple as taking a spontaneous trip over the weekend. Or going into the main city area on a weekend when all the offices are shut and showing the kids the magnificence of the historical architecture. Or a picnic to a nearby picturesque spot. And yes, do keep the phone away when you spend time with your child. Says clinical psychologist and counsellor, Sonali Gupta who works extensively with children and teens, 'In times of technology, when we are constantly available, what does take a beating is how much are we around for our children. Our ability to be mindfully available to the child both emotionally and physically, at least for the time we consciously spend with them. This adds to their stability and emotional wellbeing.'

Tell the family how proud you are of their achievements

That phone call to grandma? Or to a doting aunt? Make sure you tell them loud and clear for any little lurking ears to hear about how you are so proud that your daughter is now managing to dress herself up on her own, and how she's becoming a big, responsible girl. And of course, grandma or aunt will demand to speak to the little big girl and praise her for her mastering of getting dressed on her own, tricky buttons notwithstanding. Or that the young lad has migrated from the sippy cup to a regular glass and has a zero spill record.

Have a daily ritual with your child

It could be story time, or book reading time for an hour every day before bed. Or just sitting with your child while he or she does their home work. A simple way to celebrate your child's every day is to sit with your child for a chat every night, at bedtime, sharing what happened in your day and listening to what happened in your child's day.

Create a diary of 'I'm Proud of You' notes

In it, every time your child achieves something praise worthy, write a little note appreciating the achievement and the effort behind it. Let your child go choose the praise note diary he or she wants her notes written in. The 'I'm Proud of You' diary will also do its job when your child feels demotivated or feels he or she cannot achieve something.

Have a treat day

Celebrating a milestone no matter how simple, going diaper-free, for instance. Come to think of it, I was worried whether the child would attend his graduation ceremony in pull-ups, so much so that when he finally was potty-trained I must have cracked a tile or two cartwheeling in joy.

Key Takeaways

- Invest in creating a bank of positive memories your child can draw on when he or she feels down and out.

- Knowing that a parent cares for them, and values them can add the steel to the spine of the mildest child and every child must believe that they are important to their parents. The world is cruel enough to beat out any self-centred stuffing out of them soon enough when they get out into it, don't you worry.

- Simple every day positive celebrations are enough, you don't need an entire shebang worthy of an event management team in order to celebrate.

- All you must do is ensure their sense of self is strong enough before the world can get to them.

STEP TWO: PROTECT

Protect your child. It is a dangerous world out there and you are responsible for your child's safety.

I was a latchkey child from the age of eight. My school was almost ten kilometres from the home we shifted to after my father suddenly passed away. The school was close to my previous home and I made the trek each day by public transport, which wasn't child-friendly at all. It was a tough shift to make, especially for an eight-year-old. But my mom had rules, rules I could not dare to break. They were rules I hated. But now I realise that they were what helped me survive those years unscathed.

To begin with, she had already taught me road safety. I was crossing roads and negotiating traffic by myself by the age of six. Back then, there was no great teaching process; one walked everywhere, and crossed with one's parent, and then was expected to cross on one's own if required. Basic safety rules about walking on the pavement, crossing at a zebra crossing, checking both sides of the road before crossing, and such were already drilled into place.

One of the first rules my mom had laid down as a complete non-negotiable was that once I had entered the house, I was to not open the door to anyone except her, nor step out of the house. Nor was I, on the pain of not being bought any new books, allowed to touch the matches or the gas burner. Cold food straight from the fridge still remains my comfort food.

Of course, there were consequences to having a tween with a fertile imagination stay indoors for the better part of the day alone with only so much she could read or study. As my mom says, 'I never knew what I would find. One day I came home to you laboriously scrubbing off the steel plating from all the taps because you thought they were gold beneath. On another day, you had taken your felt pen set and drawn terrible cabbage roses over all the fabric lampshades.' Small price to pay for having me safe inside the house! The important lesson I learnt from those days was that I had to take charge of my own safety, and it is something I have tried to teach my son as well.

As a parent, perhaps the scariest thing we do most days is simply to read the newspaper. Most days will have at least one story of violence against a child, and that too, one that just makes your heartbeat accelerate, and not in a good way. Or some accident that a child was involved in, often within the home, at times, outside. A child drowning in a bucket of water. Another child falling from a balcony. A child accidentally ingesting floor cleaner.

You wonder, 'What if that was my child?' You get swamped with panic attacks. Alas, it isn't possible to keep your child manacled to your side every second of the day. You do need to gradually step back and let your child grow into a confident adult. This does mean letting your child out of your sight occasionally, never mind that you might be tempted to hire a security agency to keep a watch on her in your absence, and not to mention fit your child with a tracker and a drone camera just to be safe.

As any mother who has honked her nose tearfully through the trauma of first day at school or has sat grimly at the wheel of her car discreetly following the school bus taking her child for his first school picnic knows, letting go isn't easy. Our parents did it easier. Much easier.

When I was a child, I remember roaming the neighbourhood with my friends like a pack of hounds. There was no cell phone, no GPS, no parent by turn keeping watch duty to make sure I was in line of sight, the only thing that was mandatory was that I returned home before the street lights came on. Reaching home after the lights came on was a misdemeanour punishable by no ice cream forever and ever, a threat that kept me on the straight and narrow for years, until I figured how to reach the ice cream shop on the main road on my own.

In today's day and age, my mother would have been called negligent but she was just parenting according to her times when children were often left unsupervised and developed their own skills to navigate the world and stay out of trouble. We had nooks and crannies in our rambling compounds that we kept hidden from the adults, where we escaped to in order to do our playing. We took great pleasure in finding hidden spots, and keeping them secret. Today, our kids have sanitised play zones, rubber matted parks and CCTV surveillance. Thanks to the justified paranoia, children have no place to hide from us.

On the roads too, the traffic is infinitely worse and uncaring. While I would cross two arterial roads each time on the way to school and back on my own, I worry about the offspring doing that today, even though he is five years older than I was when I did so.

We have security guards at two levels within the apartment complex, and yet it took me almost until the child was eight to risk sending him down to play on his own. Even so, I kept calling up the security guard in the lobby of the building to keep an eye out for him. My helicopter mom mode was so high, my rotor blades got worn out.

Protecting a child is something that comes instinctively to us. Compare a human infant to most animals. A newly hatched baby turtle can make its way from the nest to the sea, with no mamma turtle alongside, gently directing the proceedings. Human babies are, in contrast, completely helplessly at birth.

Babies are cute. Nature has deliberately designed them like that in order to make us melt and want to protect them and take care of them. Their large eyes and chubby cheeks make us all feel protective towards them. An Oxford University research paper by M.L. Kringelbach titled *On Cuteness: Unlocking the Parental Brain and Beyond* says that 'Cuteness in offspring is a potent protective mechanism that ensures survival for otherwise completely dependent infants.' It's a good thing babies are so adorable, because they need years of looking after before they can survive on their own. For the first two months, they can't even lift their heads. They learn to roll over at four months, sit up at around six months and stand by approximately nine months. Then it takes another few months before they actually begin walking. Survival skills are a long way off. It is more than a decade before a human can begin to navigate the world unaided.

There was a reason nature did this. It was to allow humans to have the highly developed brains we do to manage all the requirements of our adult bodies as well as the complex reasoning, communication and language that we need. After the first decade of a child's life, the child begins puberty, a phase leading to sexual maturity, which also lasts a few years. Through all of this, a child is completely dependent upon the adults in their lives to keep them safe from harm—physical, emotional and sexual. This is a responsibility that is quite overwhelming. As a friend said, 'Sometimes I feel increasingly incapable of keeping my child safe in this world. But then, I have no choice. It is my job as a parent to put everything I can into ensuring my daughter's safety.' And then sometimes it is us who need protection from our babies. My friend and author Koral Dasgupta narrates this most hilarious anecdote from her son's first year. 'He was all of eight months, still crawling, with my mobile being his friend-of-any-hour as it never had an issue with his innate ramblings. I was the only villain who separated the "best friends". So one evening when I found him crawling towards my SOS device, I tried to get up and almost tumbled on the floor. He had wrapped the wire of the landline around my feet before approaching the mobile!'

How can we keep a child safe?

It is a huge and scary mandate. Keeping one's child safe 24/7 is a task that could challenge the most unfazed of us, and parenting at the best of times is fraught with hair being pulled out in bunches. Here are a few tips on how you can do your bit to try to make the world your child navigates a little safer for her, at home and outside.

At home

A child is safest at home, you thought? Wrong. Scarily, the home is the second most common location for fatalities amongst children. Who amongst us doesn't have a scary story from our own childhood, or about our own kids: a head stuck into a grill, a swallowed coin, a small detachable part of a toy pushed into a nostril or even cleaning fluid drunk straight from the bottle by a crawling child who mistakes it for milk. Minor burns, cuts and scrapes aside, to the more real and terrifying dangers of poisoning, drowning or electrical shocks can happen at home even if one has one's eyes out on stalks and swivelling around to prevent them from happening. The American comedian Milton Berle wisely asked, 'If evolution really works, how come mothers only have two hands?'

Incidentally, falls, poisoning and fires and burns are the leading cause of injuries caused in the home. This is followed by choking or suffocation. Sometimes even two inches of water can be dangerous for little children. But you can childproof your home and protect your child. When the offspring moved from flipping himself to his stomach to crawling with skates on his knees through the house, the first thing we had to do was to get the home childproofed, and it was then that we realised how the most innocuous things could actually be hazardous to a child. The razor edge of the marble coffee table, the bars of the box grill, the open electrical sockets, the magnetic doors to the bathrooms, all became potential dangers.

Here are a few tips to keep in mind while childproofing the home:

- The easiest way to realise what could be a potential hazard for your baby is to get down to the baby's eye level and crawl around. You will see table edges, drawers, cupboards, spaces under beds, sharp corners, etc. in a new light when you do.
- As your child begins walking, you would need to do another round at a higher level.
- Tape up all electric points which aren't being used with duct tape. Use outlet caps on those that are.
- Make sure all dangerous and potentially hazardous things like detergents, cleaning products, medications,

sharp objects like knives and forks are kept at a height out of reach for your baby.

- Don't let the baby into the kitchen, even if it is for a moment. Have a play pen you can put your baby in, with soft toys, at a spot you can keep an eye on her if you need to work in the kitchen.
- Tiny objects are always a danger, so watch out for things like decorative stones, pebbles, hair clips, etc. that your child could reach out for and pop into his or her mouth.
- Consider padding and rounding sharp edges of furniture that could be at eye level for a boisterous toddler.
- Have a gate with a difficult latch that stops toddlers from going out of the front door if it is left open inadvertently. If you have a home with a stair case you might want to install a gate at the top of the stairs to prevent your baby from crawling down the stairs.
- Rid your home of rugs that slip or put anti-slip underlay to prevent them from slipping, carpet your stairs if you have them in your home. Put handrails on the side of the stairs. In bathrooms, have non-slip bathmats and grab rails wherever needed. Invest in night lights.
- Make sure all cleaning products are out of reach of children. Label all unmarked liquid containers. Don't reuse food containers to store cleaning materials. Keep your medicines out of reach. Keep the number of your paediatrician or the nearest hospital on speed dial on your phone and written in big letters on a post it stuck to your kitchen soft board or refrigerator.

- Keep plastic bags, strings, ropes etc. out of reach.
- Make sure little children have food that is cut up into bite-sized pieces or is soft enough to be swallowed easily.
- Don't let water run when you're not around. Switch off geysers, don't use gadgets near water and keep toilet lids closed.
- Install smoke detectors. Don't leave your kitchen unsupervised when you have the flame lit.

Keeping your child safe outside the home

This could be perhaps the most challenging, but is also the most necessary because while you can have some amount of control over what your child encounters at home, the world outside is a place your child will eventually have to deal with. Here's what you must do to empower your child to stay safe while out of the home.

- Insist your child memorises your full name, phone numbers and address as soon as he or she can, in case he ever gets lost.
- As soon as your child can understand colours, teach your child how to negotiate traffic signals, about red, green and orange lights. If your child can count, show your child how the number across shows her how many seconds she has before the traffic in that lane begins moving. Teach your child about zebra crossings. Basic rules like looking at the side of oncoming traffic as well as the side she is on, crossing only when traffic has come to a complete halt,

holding one's hand out while crossing the road. Do keep crossing roads with your child as often as you can, while explaining what they need to do, until your child learns.

- Make sure you have a code word or a phrase that only you and your child know, which you will pass on to only a trusted adult in case you are unable to pick him up from school.
- Insist that your child informs you if there is any change of schedule or if he or she is out unsupervised.
- Explain the risk of accepting things or food items from strangers.
- Instruct your child about what they should do if they're ever separated from you in a crowded place. They should find a person in authority—a policeman, a mall attendant, or go to the staff at the checkout counter in a store, let them know they're lost and ask for an announcement to be made for you, or for the staff to call you if the child knows your number by heart.
- It is always a good thing to make little children who cannot memorise numbers wear little wristbands with their names, your contact numbers and residential address if you are going out to a crowded place, where they could get separated from you.
- Avoid giving your child any item of clothing with their name visible on it from a distance. Sometimes predators use names they read off a bag or a jacket to create a familiarity with a trusting child.

- Tell a child they are never ever to get into a car with someone they don't know, no matter what that person tells them, and that it is okay to say no and create a scene to avoid doing so.

Keeping a child safe from sexual predators

Apart from teaching a child how to navigate the world within the home and without with alertness and care, as a parent, a prime responsibility you have is to equip your child with the vocabulary and the agency over his or her body to help them deter sexual predators. For four years I, along with a team of dear friends and volunteers, ran an online social media initiative called Child Sexual Abuse (CSA) Awareness Month, to spread information about the prevalence of CSA and to break the silence around it, as well as to tell parents about what they could do to empower their children to recognise and understand potential danger.

My son, has, from the time he's been old enough to name his body parts, known that his private parts and anyone else's private parts are off-limits and he is to keep in mind the three magic words, 'No. Stop. Tell.'

This is basically what I call a first line of defence one can teach a child against anything that makes him uncomfortable. First, he is to say 'no', loudly and clearly. Secondly, he is to tell the person to stop, and, thirdly, he is to say that he will tell his parents about it. Hopefully, this would deter some predators. I've also taught him agency over his body. It is okay if he doesn't feel like hugging a particular adult; he has the right to say 'no'. Needless to say, this has led to some awkward situations when my mom, his doting grandma, has wanted a hug and kiss, and he's been in a 'IDonWantu' mood. I hope it keeps him safe.

The biggest myth going around is that CSA perpetrators are strangers in a dark alley, but in fact, the majority of sexual crimes against children are committed by people they know and trust and, most importantly, have unfettered access to them.

How then, can you keep your children safe from sexual predators? Here are a few points to keep in mind from Dr Manjeer Mukherjee Director—Training, Research and Development at arpan.org, an organisation that does stellar work in the space of CSA awareness.

- **Get involved**: Get involved in your child's life as there is no substitute for your attention and supervision. Be aware of your children's environment, the programmes they watch on television or the internet, the kind of games they play both virtually and in the real world. We can let our children know what is going on in our lives and find out what they are up to. It will help build healthy relationships, and let them know we care.

- **Respect the child's feelings**: Respect the child's feelings and their likes and dislikes around touches. Support, encourage and praise your child for sharing his thoughts and feelings. Avoid discouraging statements and labels.

- **Be aware**: Aware parents and caretakers can help protect as well as respond better to sexual abuse. Know more about the issue, the signs and symptoms of an abusive situation, ways to prevent, support and seek help. Be articulate about your discomfort, if any. Seek resources and help. This will help you be comfortable with the necessary vocabulary of private body parts and sexual abuse.

- **Teach personal safety**: Teach your children about personal safety as you are their best teacher. Teach names of private body parts, identification of safe and unsafe touches as well as personal safety rules. The key personal safety rules are: 'It is NEVER all right for someone to touch, look or talk about your private body parts except to keep them clean and healthy. It is never alright for someone older or bigger to ask you to touch, look or talk about their private body parts. If someone tries to break this rule, say 'No' and 'Get away'. Tell someone you trust and keep telling until you get the help you need. These messages can be articulated in an age-appropriate way, for example, with young children the vocabulary can be of rules; for pre-teens it can be around guidelines whereas for adolescents it can be around action points. Just like we teach our children safety rules about crossing the road, we should also teach them about safe and unsafe touches.

- **Talk 'the talk'**: There is no magic age at which you can have 'the talk' around personal safety. But it is a good idea to have many talks. It is best to talk with your child from a young age in an age appropriate manner so that it does not come as a surprise or shame. If your child knows what to expect ahead of time, the changes that come with growing up will be easier to deal with. Some parents wait until their child asks questions. If your child is shy, or does not ask questions, or has a sense of shame about their private body parts, you may have to take the lead. If you have not started these conversations yet, do not hesitate to start talking about them. It is never too late to talk to them about it. If they do not get information from you, there is a high possibility that they will look for it someplace else. The information they find may be inappropriate and confusing. This increases their vulnerability as others can take advantage of them.

- **Answer children**: Answer children's questions honestly and factually. Children are curious and ask a lot of questions; they are growing and are exposed to so many new things every day. When children raise questions, we need to give them honest responses in an age appropriate manner. At these times, it is important not to be angry with the child or show embarrassment or prevent the child from asking such questions or to ignore the question. Parents can look for resources that can help them be more comfortable to answer children factually in an age-appropriate manner. Parents can also let their children know if they do not have an answer to their question at that time. It then becomes the parent's responsibility to find out the answer and let the child know. The parents should neither treat this as an excuse to avoid the question nor should they wait for the children to ask it for the second time.

- **Listen:** Talk goes both ways. A good way to encourage children to talk is to be an active listener; do not appear to judge the child or what happened. Encourage them to tell if something unsafe is happening or if someone is behaving in a way that scares them. Let them know they can tell or ask for help from you and other adults.
- **Stay calm:** Speak to your child in a calm and reassuring way as fear is not an effective teaching tool, but confidence is.

Key Takeaways

- Childproof your home from the time your child begins crawling.
- Keep updating the childproofing as your child grows and begins walking.
- Teach your child how to be safe in a public situation.
- Equip your child with the self-confidence, sense of agency over his or her body and the comfort to tell you anything to help them deter sexual predators.

STEP THREE: NOURISH

Food for the body, food for the mind and food for the soul.

Only when all aspects of the child's needs are met can a child grow to become a mature human being.

The tale of Abhimanyu is something most of us are familiar with. According to the Mahabharata, Arjuna's son Abhimanyu, could successfully break through the Chakravyuha, a complicated and dangerous spiral battle formation. As the story goes, he was able to do this because he had heard his father narrate the technique to his mother, who was pregnant with him at that time. Unfortunately, Abhimanyu's mother did not hear the exit strategy. The result was that Abhimanyu sadly perished in the process. What this tale from myth does tell us is what research now confirms after having studied the environment within the womb with probes and scans: the unborn child can be influenced by the world outside the womb and can hear the voices of those outside it.

According to the Vedas, a pregnant woman should ensure that she is in a positive state of mind, emotionally, mentally and spiritually. She should be physically well-nourished and comfortable. Listening to music, thinking positive thoughts, eating healthy, praying and meditating and communicating with one's unborn child are the most important elements. According to the Mayo Clinic, a baby develops the ability to hear in the womb at about eighteen weeks into the pregnancy. According to some experts, listening to music will stimulate your baby's brain development and sense of hearing. A study conducted by Vivekananda Yoga Research Foundation in Bangalore, in 2005, found that pregnant women who enrolled in a yoga programme that included breathing exercises and meditation were likely to have heavier birth weight babies and were less likely to go into labour prematurely. Therefore, nourishing a child begins right from the stage of conception itself, and not from when the child is born into the world.

When I was pregnant with the offspring, I remember feeling much like a passive receptacle of everything being fed into me. The mother and the mother-in-law hovered around in the background dishing up the most appetising food ever, never mind the all-pervasive morning sickness that followed no rules about sticking to the morning. Then there was the 'read positive spiritual things and watch happy movies' dictum that one followed for the entire nine months one was incubator to the offspring. I must confess though, I was kept away kicking and screaming from watching *The Lord of the Rings* when it was being telecast during my pregnancy by my mother, who took one look at the Orcs from Sauron's army and decided that her grandchild in the making would not be exposed to these creatures. Instead, she fed me a steady diet of positive and happy television shows, including *Friends*, on a loop, which probably could explain why the offspring is perma-glued onto the couch most days and has to be physically peeled off and put to bed.

I realised then, that it was important to nourish the child from the time the child came into existence and this was way before the child even emerged into the world. There is, of course, a scientific explanation for this. The food a mother eats is what will nourish the foetus, and food that is nutritious will assist foetal development. The state of mind the mother is in through the pregnancy will affect the child. In fact, there is even a term for it—'Garbh Sanskar'—or the impressions in the womb. Across cultures, pregnancy has a lot of taboos associated with it. From not looking at the moon during an eclipse, to not stepping out of the house to avoid evil spirits, to not looking at dead bodies, to name just a few. While one may choose to follow or disregard these views, it cannot be denied that a foetus is constantly getting messages from its mother. Not just the auditory signals from her voice and her heartbeat above it, but also chemical signals from the placenta in the womb. A study published in *Psychological Science*, a journal of the Association for Psychological Science, found that if the mother was depressed, it affected the development of the baby after it was born.

A child, within the womb—and when it emerges into the environment—soaks up everything it can get from it. A child needs nourishment of all kinds, from food to mental and emotional stimulation. All these given in adequate doses will ensure that a child's physical, mental and emotional growth is not stunted, and that all happen in tandem.

Nourishing your child with the right food

Nourishing a child with food begins early, right from what one eats during the pregnancy, as I realised much to my dismay, being compelled to eat all kinds of healthy, wholesome, home cooked food when I was pregnant, and having to cut out the alcohol and the junk food. Once the baby is born, the debate begins about breast milk versus formula, and then the induced guilt if one is unable to produce enough breast milk to help the baby grow adequately and is compelled to supplement or switch to formula. And after we've finished beating ourselves up over it, we deal with picky eaters, food jags, the treatment of vegetables as outlaws on the dinner plates to be roundly ignored, the obsessions with colas, the dangerous flirtations with burgers. Food is a minefield a parent tiptoes across every single day. So how do you ensure your child eats healthy?

Trying to get a picky eater to eat a meal before grass begins growing under their feet is a test that many parents are familiar with. As anyone who has pulled out chunks of hair in the valiant attempt at getting their kids to eat will tell you, kids and food have a difficult equation. They will either be such fussy eaters that one frets about them getting their requisite doses of vitamins and minerals that are needed to grow; or it could possibly be the reverse, where they are such indiscriminate eaters that you will be literally reining them in to stop them tipping the weighing scales into childhood obesity.

Be a healthy eater yourself

Ensuring that your child eats healthy begins at home, and with you. A parent is perhaps the most important influence in a child's food habits. Children not only learn table manners from you but also cues on nutrition and healthy eating. Your relationship with food is what your child will grow up with and emulate. If your child sees you pussyfooting the veggies on your plate to the far edge while you thunder at him to down those greens, you're not going to convince him that eating them is good for him. So eat your greens, have your five helpings of fruit and vegetables every single day, and hope he learns by example, and a little motivation.

Learn from the French

The French are a nation that eats healthy and inculcates the habit of eating healthy in their kids, right from the time they are very young. How do they manage to do that, you wonder, while you're invoking every birdie and ghostie in the immediate periphery to get each morsel down the offspring's throat? Here's what Pamela Druckerman, the author of *Bringing Up Bebe, One American Mother Discovers the Wisdom of French Parenting*, says. 'French parents see it as their job to bring the child around to appreciating this food. They believe that just as they must teach a child how to sleep, how to wait, and how to say bonjour, they must teach her how to eat.' In Mei Ling Hopgood's book, *How Eskimos Keep their Babies Warm: Parenting Wisdom from Around the World*, she speaks about her experience in a French class room, where children are actually excited to eat boiled beans, cheese and fruit for dessert. The trick, according to her, is that the French get their kids involved in the food from the preparation stage. She writes, 'I took to heart what I was hearing from French families: if you value your food and food time then your child will. If eating is simply something you have to do, between everything else you have to cram in your day, that is probably how your child will think as well.'

Here's what they do, and how we can learn from them:

- Stick to three main meals a day, with one after school snack. The French don't encourage mid-meal snacking because that kills appetite come meal time.

- Have a hearty meal that includes a starter, a main course, cheese and dessert. Opt for generous portions that would keep hunger at bay between meals. A dessert isn't necessarily something sweet, it could just be a fruit.

- Ensure that the child drinks water. Along with meals and between meals.

- Make it a point to sit down at the table and eat. Meals are to be eaten with pleasure and care, and not something you do distractedly in front of the television or any other screen. Turn off all gadgets during meals as a rule.

- Eat light for dinner. Make lunch the main meal of the day, with dinner a light soup or salad with yoghurt or fruit for dessert.
- Learn to recognise when you are full, and stop when you are.
- Don't gobble down your food, but taste and enjoy it. Discuss the ingredients of the food you are eating; the cooking process gets the children involved in the conversation.
- Have a strict 'no snacking after dinner' rule. Once you're done with dinner, that's it. No midnight foraging in the refrigerator.
- Get your older child to help you with the preparation and cooking of a meal. Of course, supervise them handling sharp knives or open flames. A younger child can help with the prep, washing of the ingredients, cleaning things, peeling, etc. as well as accompany you to the market to shop for ingredients. It makes them curious about the ingredients and the cooking process.

Interestingly, France has one of the lowest rates of childhood obesity amongst developed nations. Food, in French culture, is associated with pleasure and not guilt. The French also make sure their children eat the same food that adults do, and that the maximum part of their meal comprises a broad range of dishes that includes meat, dairy and fresh vegetables, as well as fruits. Instead of milk, children eat cheese or yoghurt, and drink primarily water. Children also learn early about limiting portion sizes. The entire approach to food is positive. While there is the positive of knowing why a particular food item is good for you, enjoying eating it is more impactful when it comes to making it a meal choice.

Make the most of family meal times

A research team from Rutgers, the State University of New Jersey found that kids who ate more meals together with their families tended to eat more fruits, vegetables, fibre, calcium-rich foods, and vitamins, and also ate less junk food.

Family mealtimes are your opportunity to teach your child healthy food habits. Walk the talk applies at the dining table as well as in all other aspects of life. Keep encouraging your child to taste new things, it takes an average of seven times before a taste becomes agreeable to someone. In fact make it a rule that a new dish has to be tried at least three times. Psst, the taste will grow on them in three tries. Even something as foul-tasting as Chyawanprash has grown on the offspring with putting it down the hatch every day; he can now swallow a spoonful without flinching.

Include healthy ingredients in everyday meals and snacks

Make breakfast an important meal. It is a pity if the first meal of the day is a hurried affair with something like cereal dunked in cold milk. Inculcate the habit of a proper breakfast, with good proteins like eggs, lean meats or cottage cheese and if you are a vegetarian, traditional Indian breakfasts like idli-sambar-chutney, or poha, paratha or chillas are all healthy and nutritionally sound. While most kids don't have the time to have breakfast at home because they need to run to catch the school bus, make sure they have a healthy tiffin box packed for their snack time. Try and make most meals from fresh produce, as much as time and convenience permits. In India, we still thankfully do, in most homes, make fresh meals from scratch and aren't as dependent on frozen dinners and takeaways as the West.

A growing child needs adequate sources of protein from both animal and vegetable sources, so do include dairy products, lean meats, soya, eggs, yoghurt for probiotics, green leafy vegetables, beans, lentils and nuts in their diet. Be sure to include nuts and seeds to give your child protein, iron, zinc and phosphorus and fatty acids. Nuts like almonds give your child Vitamin E while Brazil nuts give a power dose of selenium. Teach your kid to snack on a handful of nuts, veggie sticks or salads rather than packaged snacks when they feel peckish.

Get your child into the kitchen

Don't make the kitchen this mysterious space that only parents or adults are allowed into, where cooked food emerges as mysteriously as though cooked by Dobby and the elves. Demystify the kitchen for the child. Make your child help a bit with the basic preparations, cleaning, washing, shelling peas, sorting stuff. A child feels most chuffed at being entrusted with some responsibility, and you never know, your little sous chef could one day find a passion for food that goes professional. Even if that doesn't happen, it always helps if a child has enough basic kitchen skills to feed himself when an adult is not around. Making a sandwich for instance. Get your child to give his or her inputs on the menu for the one meal you eat as a family, dinner perhaps. Cooking is a life skill, and knowing how to rustle up an edible meal will always come in handy in the long run.

Another neat trick to get a child more involved with food and its ingredients is to create a little kitchen garden and get your child involved with the planting and growing of little herbs or whatever convenient to the space you live in and the climate you have. Children have a sense of involvement with something they've grown and might just be more inclined to eat a carrot they've raised from scratch than something bought from a vendor.

Dealing with a picky eater

Coercing a child to eat a healthy range of foods, trying to go beyond the standard two or three acceptable items, or even to make a child just eat can make the most sanguine parent morph into a dead ringer for Attila the Hun. While some parents like celebrity chef Curtis Stone advocate letting fussy eaters go hungry and to keep re-serving what has been refused, you might just quail at the thought of letting your child go hungry. Perhaps there is perhaps a middle road you could opt for.

Picky eating as a phase generally peaks around eighteen months. Often, it is an individual child's temperament that mandates how a child responds to new foods. Sometimes picky eating could be due to lack of exposure to different food textures, lumpy foods, or delayed oral motor skills like chewing or the ability to move food in the mouth. If this is the case and this causes gagging, it could in turn lead to further fear of food. If you've force-fed your child in desperation to get some nutrition down the hatch, you might make the child incapable of regulating their hunger, and cause them to lose their appetite.

If your child will only eat mashed potatoes or spend hours pushing a single morsel to every extremity of her mouth, reducing you to a blubbering mass of entreaties, following her around the premises brandishing a spoon garnished with pleas and dire threats, you might worry, and with good cause, about whether your child is getting adequate nutrition to fuel growth. But, here's what you could do to deal with a picky eater.

- Firstly, don't use compulsion, coercion or bribes to get your child to eat. It just turns meal times into pitched battle scenes and creates unnecessary anxiety over food that should in actuality be a pleasurable time.
- Sometimes, picky eating could be caused by role models like yourself, who could be eating only certain fixed foods without realising it. Have you looked at your own plate recently?
- Serve smaller portions, so your child can control how much he or she really wants.
- Have a routine in place, so your child knows when it is meal time.

- Don't allow your child to load up on the between meal snacks, which can quite kill appetite.
- Introduce new foods along with old favourites.
- Encourage your child to try out new food, and don't worry if your child doesn't take to it immediately. Keep reintroducing it.
- Use dips and sauces to make food more appealing, use colourful foods to pique interest, turn off gadgets during meals and don't make dessert a prize to be withheld if the food on your child's plate is not finished. Instead, make dessert about healthy eating, like fruit for instance, or a flavoured yoghurt.
- Don't make a separate meal for your child if he or she doesn't want to eat what is made for the entire family. Instead, try and convince your child to try a little of what is served.
- And yes, if the picky eating persists for a while and worries you, do consult your paediatrician for supplements your child could take if needed.

Dealing with food jags

The offspring has had his share of food jags. When he was still in diapers and had but little vocabulary, he would demand 'EggieKhachKhach' (scrambled eggs) every day at every meal until I could feel the eggie coming out of my ears. In troth my melted brain.

As a pre-schooler, his standard tantrum of one per day was for the dratted 'Vunchickabuggawidcheese' (one chicken burger with cheese). The tantrums were so horrendous for a hapless first-time mom to deal with, that more often than not, I would cave in and call for the damned 'chickabuggawidcheese' or take him to the nearest outlet with them golden arches. The high point of his day, I think, was standing nose at counter height, and piping up loudly for his happy—and my unhappy—meal from the bemused attendant and handing over the requisite amount with an expression that bordered on the direly threatening. Thankfully he grew out of that phase soon enough, and now has a burger only under duress when travelling by road where the only place on the highway without roaches on steroids seem to be the proverbial golden arches, and hence safe for ingestion.

I agonised then, harassed my hapless paediatrician and weighed my son after every meal agonising about stunted growth and deficiencies as spewed by Google baba. After all, what is a mom for if not to trip up over guilt and smash her nose in every single day. Food jags are nasty demons. Sometimes, kids can go on for weeks or even months eating the same thing, and this could prevent them from getting all the nutrients they need for growth. Kids can drive you quite insane, and I concur with Sam Levinson when he said, 'Insanity is hereditary: You can get it from your children.'

Why do kids have food jags, you wonder? With very young kids, it could be caused by poor oral motor development, which makes chewing difficult, or they could have some sensory issues related to other food, in their taste, touch or even smell. If your child hasn't been encouraged to try out new foods regularly, there might be a reluctance to try new foods. If some food has caused tummy aches and upsets, a child might unconsciously reject all food, except what he or she feels safe with. And food is comforting, sometimes, a food jag is nothing but an extended play of opting for comfort food. As a parent, you would naturally worry that your child might suffer from poor nutrition, and meal times might be ticking bombs in terms of stress and getting them to try new foods.

How you could deal with food jags is to ensure the same food is not offered in a row, making the same item in different ways. For instance, an egg could be offered scrambled, poached or fried to create a sense of variety. Don't get worked up over meal times, and offer a couple of options apart from the food item your kid is currently obsessed with. Perhaps you could coerce them to eat those in addition to the one they are fixated with. And try to eat a meal with your child; when your child sees you eating a selection of things, he or she might just be tempted to reach out and try something he'd been rejecting before.

Nourishing the mind

Perhaps the greatest miracle one can ever witness in one's lifetime is one that we all take so much for granted, namely, the development of a child from a newborn to an adult. The brain of a newborn contains around 100 billion neurons which will eventually make connections via synapses and help the child learn things. These connections, and the consequent learning will happen only when there is enough positive stimuli in the child's environment.

According to *The Tibetan Art of Parenting: From Before Conception Through Early Childhood,* by Anne Maiden Brown, PhD, psychotherapist and social psychologist, a child's mind is naturally simple before it gets developmentally able to relate present and past experiences, with its senses, thoughts and emotions. To quote Maria Montessori, early childhood educationist, 'The most important period of life is not the age of university studies, but the first one, the period from birth to the age of six.' It is at this stage that we need to be most aware of how we nourish the child's mind.

Emotional nourishment

Did you know that the infant brain is unfinished? The relationship of the child with his caretakers and his interaction with the world outside is what will mould his brain wiring in the next few years. At birth, every child has a brain that still has to develop the parts handling emotional and social behaviour, as well as thinking. As a consequence, relationships and experiences with parents and people around them is what will influence a child's brain development. Even if your child has yet to speak his or her first word, the brain is growing at its fastest, tripling in size. Before your child is five years old, he or she has done a lot of learning.

One-on-one interaction

When a mother coos to her baby, looking into her eyes, when a father plays with his toddler, every activity that is a positive, loving interaction affects the brain and its consequent development. These are just regular everyday interactions, but what they provide to a child is the critical emotional nourishment needed to promote brain development. Simple things like touching, rocking, talking, singing, smiling, all help babies understand the world around, and feel cared for and cherished.

When a baby cries, he or she is expressing some distress that needs to be taken care of and calmed down. A response from a parent or a caregiver with comfort, or food, will turn off the stress in the baby's brain and the baby will calm down, creating brain cell networks to help the baby learn to soothe himself. A conversation in gibberish would be what your speaking and words sound like to your baby initially, but babies pick up words and sound patterns and hearing these repeatedly help the brain parts handling speech and language develop. Use every opportunity you can to speak with a baby, even if the baby can't reply to you just yet. Soon enough, the gurgles back to you will morph into clearly enunciated words. Allowing your child to explore and play, yet be there for them when they need you also helps them learn in a secure environment.

Limit screen time

The American Academy of Paediatrics does not recommend screen time at all for children under two. But, sadly, gadgets with screens have become all pervasive demons in most homes and, more often than not, get used as reliable babysitters by most of us when we're just craving some down time. The other day I was at a competitive sporting event for children, and to my dismay found all the kids emerge from their event, and sink into a gadget—a tablet, an iPad, a phone. None of them were really interacting with each other or their parents. It made me sad that they had retreated so far into the virtual world that basic interaction with the very real folk around them was an effort.

Research conducted by child-education specialists at the Michael Cohen Group shows that touch screens have now taken over all other forms of entertainment for children. 60 per cent of parents with children under twelve said their kids play often on touch screens and 38 per cent put it at 'very often.' Interestingly, 36 per cent of the children in this survey had their own device. The scene isn't very different in urban India. Another research conducted by the Kaiser Family Foundation found that 8-18 year-olds spent an average of 7.5 hours on entertainment media in a day. A friend confessed that when she came home after a long day at work, her toddler ran to her arms outstretched demanding not a hug, but rather her phone. Another friend confesses that she's terrified of taking the iPad away from her five year old because of the rage he flies into.

You might think having a kid glued to a screen might seem like a welcome babysitter when you need to get work done without sticky hands hanging onto your legs demanding your attention. But here's why you should worry. Children who are exposed to a lot of screen time are passive receptacles of stimuli, both visual and auditory. They do not learn the business of childhood, namely curiosity-driven play, social interaction with peers, and by extension, how to navigate the real world. This eventually would impact, in variable ways, their communication, social and behavioural skills and growth. Bear in mind that overexposure to gadgets has been linked to attention deficit, cognitive delays and impaired learning.

In an interview with a British newspaper, Bill Gates, the founder of Microsoft, revealed that he and his wife Melinda rigorously limited their children's exposure to devices, prohibiting them from owning a cell phone before they turned fourteen or using their devices at dinner time. 'We often set a time after which there is no screen time and in their case that helps them get to sleep at a reasonable hour,' he told the newspaper. According to the *New York Times*, Steve Jobs, the founder of Apple, also kept devices to a minimum for his kids.

When children watch television and video games, the part of the brain that is connected with decision making, problem solving and analysis, namely the cortex, is under stimulated. Instead, what does get stimulated is the low and mid brain areas. An average of three to five hours of television watching can eventually lead to a decrease in focus and concentration, a loss of ability to engage oneself in meaningful activities, perhaps a language delay and diminished vocabulary. And we're not even talking about the other deluge of screens children are bombarded with, from mobile phones to tablets. A good idea would be to begin weaning your child off gadgets, limiting screen time, getting them outdoors and playing in the open, if you can. Interestingly, this addiction to gadgets amongst children has also given rise to a new term, 'iPaddy,' which is a term coined for kids who throw violent tantrums when their electronic devices are confiscated.

There are a slew of different things a child can do with his or her time. For one, take a child outdoors as much as you can. Spending time amidst nature is a learning experience no amount of videos and simulated games can ever replicate. To quote Maria Montessori, 'Let the children be free; encourage them; let them run outside when it is raining; let them remove their shoes when they find a puddle of water; and when the grass of the meadows is wet with dew, let them run on it and trample it with their bare feet; let them rest peacefully when a tree invites them to sleep beneath its shade; let them shout and laugh when the sun wakes them in the morning.'

Spending time in the outdoors is always good for children because they can use all their five senses, which cannot happen whilst focused on a screen. To quote Shakespeare from *As You Like It*, your child will 'Find tongues in trees, books in running brooks, sermons in stones, and good in everything.'

Get them reading

My father died when I was less than nine. My memories of him are blurred and indistinct, but what I do remember very clearly are the books he read out to me as a baby. Every evening, after he returned from a long day at work, through the grind of public transport from one end of the city's commercial hub to the boondocks of the suburbs, he would take me on his lap and read to me. Picture books, of course. Pretty soon, I am told by the proud mater, I began reading back to him. Of course, it wasn't reading but mere picture word association, but to me it was a grown-up thing to do and I persisted.

While other parents would buy their children toys, my father would take me to the bookstore and unleash me in that wonderland of paper and print. I remember, that despite his rather humble earnings as a bank clerk, he would never flinch at the cost of any book I chose. Thanks to him, I actually began my first entrepreneurial venture at the age of seven by creating my own home library, which earned me enough pocket money to keep me in tooth-rotting sweets without my mother's permission.

I often wonder if I would have ended up an author had my father not sowed the love of books in me when I was a baby. On the flipside though, I must confess, my son has not taken to reading no matter how much I tried, and that has been my one big regret.

Why is it important to get a child to read, you might ask?

For one, it improves their vocabulary and imagination. For another, it develops skill with language and speech skills.

This in turn is advantageous academically, because the child is familiar with words and sentence structures, and will have better logical skills. Reading also creates empathy and educates a child about unfamiliar places, cultures and situations. Most importantly, and a boon in this era of children who can't seem to sit still in one place, reading helps a child develop focus and concentration. Reading to very young children, according to research, is strongly correlated with brain activation in areas connected with visual imagery and understanding language.

To help your child develop a love for books it isn't enough to hand him or her a book and expect it to be pored over. If your child is anything like my son was as a baby, the book will be shredded to pieces and the remnants danced over with hobnailed boots. To inculcate the reading habit, you could try making a bedtime story a daily ritual a child looks forward to. Read so your child can see the text and run your finger along the words printed so your child follows the text as you say the words. Slowly, your child will begin understanding the meaning of the words, and want to read her own books. Have books scattered around your home and let your child see you reading. A lot. And from there, hopefully, you will have eventually created a little reader.

Create curiosity

We all know of Albert Einstein as one of the greatest scientists of all time. Interestingly, he started speaking late and when he finally did, it was in full sentences. When asked why he didn't speak earlier, he replied that he had never felt the need to. Einstein was also considered a slow learner. One of his teachers did remark, rather unkindly, that he would never make anything of himself (we can only imagine how this teacher would have had to salt his words when eventually forced to eat them).

When he was around five, his father got him a compass. This was perhaps, a turning point for the young Einstein. It fascinated him that no matter how the compass was turned, the needle would always point towards the north. This fascination let him to understand the concept of magnetic fields, a quest that led on to him becoming one of the greatest theoretical physicists of the modern era. One never knows what quite gets the cogs and wheels in a child's cranial circuitry whirring.

Another interesting story is that of Thomas Edison. We know him as perhaps one of the most prolific inventors of modern times, but his teachers labelled him a slow learner and his mother was compelled to take him out of school and home school him because the school did not want him. In fact, Edison was anything but a slow learner. Studying from home, made him a voracious reader, reading across subjects, sparking his curiosity about things. One day, his father introduced him to a book by the philosopher Thomas Paine which led him to read more on philosophy, which in turn led him to be more questioning about things. Not being completely schooled in a formal education system led him to be more curious and seek out information of interest to him. This slow learner went on to invent, among other things, the electric bulb and the phonograph.

Not all learning must happen in school. A substantial amount of learning happens at home. As Raymond S. Moore says in his book, *School Can Wait*, 'An alarming number of parents appear to have little confidence in their ability to "teach" their children. We should help parents understand the overriding importance of incidental teaching in the context of warm, consistent companionship. Such caring is usually the greatest teaching, especially if caring means sharing in the activities of the home.'

The bottom line is that as parents, our job is to expose our children to as many different experiences and influences as we can. While the mania of flash carding infants till their earliest memories of their parents' faces would be a flashcard stating 'A for Apple' might seem a trifle extreme, a parent can only do good by picking up cues about what interests a child and feeding that interest with information, resources and if required, professional training. Malcolm Gladwell in his book, *Outliers*, speaks about the benefits of what he calls 'concerted cultivation'. He writes about a young boy called Alex, who '... gets taken to museums and gets enrolled in special programs and goes to summer camp, where he takes classes. When he's bored at home, there are plenty of books to read, and his parents see it as their responsibility to keep him actively engaged in the world around him. It's not hard to see how Alex would get better at reading and math over the summer.'

Nurture creativity

All mankind's greatest leaps have come from curious and creative minds. When you invest in a child's curiosity, you also must encourage creativity. Children are not only innately curious, but this innate curiosity feeds an innate creativity that does not confine itself to the tried and tested norms. To quote Einstein, 'Imagination is more important than knowledge.' How then can you nourish creativity and imagination in your child? Taking your child outdoors, as I mentioned earlier, is a great way to encourage imagination and creativity. One of my favourite games I played as a child was to look at passing clouds, imagine what they could be and build entire narratives in my head as to what was playing out in the sky above me. When my teachers complained that I always had my head in the clouds, they weren't too far off the mark. Play word games with your child. Teach them how to garden, show them how things grow. Encourage them to write out their own skits and stage them. Encourage them to make things, arts and crafts, hobby sets, best out of waste… There's no need for formal art and craft classes.Let the child dabble in what interests him. If there is a spark, the child will drive his or her learning through more formal training. Making things is a powerful way to let a child's imagination flow free. Play tell-a-story, where you begin a story and pass the thread along to see how it develops. Invest in taking them to plays and art galleries, museums, and storytelling sessions at bookstores.

Nourish your child's soul

While food for the mind and body is all too important, very often we put food for the soul on the backburner. Whether you are religious and/or spiritual or not, feeding a child's soul is definitely something that is integral to the well being of the child. It begins with something as simple as helping a child be in touch with his or her feelings. When children are young, they don't have a filter at all, they cry when they're hungry or upset or hurt, they laugh when something delights them, they say what comes to their mind instantly without weighing whether they should say so or not. It is over the years, and living with folks around, that makes them wary of truly expressing their feelings. But feelings are important. As Rudolf Steiner says in *How to Know Higher Worlds*, 'Feelings are for the soul what food is for the body.' A child in touch with his or her soul, will automatically have an inner moral compass that should see him or her through the most conflicting decisions. According to psychologist Tobin Hart, the author of *The Secret Spiritual World of Children*, children innately have a sense of love, compassion, awe and wonder, as well as moments of wisdom without rituals or training. As parents, it is one of our responsibilities to teach our children empathy, concern for other human beings, to love and respect all living beings and to have a strong moral compass for good and bad. Teaching your child how to be spiritual doesn't necessarily mean religion, it could be the simplest of things like learning to share their toys without rancour, being helpful to the elderly or the differently-abled and learning contentment and gratitude for all they have.

The offspring's earliest lessons in giving began when he was very young. After a certain number of toys had been reached, he had to weed out some and give them away to children who had no toys. The first time we did this was after a birthday, when he'd been inundated with enough and more toys as gifts. We took him with us when we gave the toys and clothes he'd outgrown (all in impeccable condition, I assure you), and the visit left a lasting impression on him. Eventually, he would himself begin keeping aside brand new toys and books he received to give away. 'I hab lots and enuff,' he would declare.

Teaching a child to wait for something they really want and earning it through saving and achieving targets could also be a spiritual lesson in itself, delayed gratification is the bulwark of endurance and tolerance. I've been guilty of succumbing to the whine-whine-whine that the offspring, with the innate manipulativeness most kids come hardwired with, did to get me to buy what he wanted, and I've regretted it. I'm an older mom, and twenty minutes hardboiled an egg when it comes to dealing with whining now. He waits for what he wants, and has targets set to warrant getting it. It makes him appreciate better what he gets.

Another way to impart spiritual lessons is storytelling. Tales from myth and history with a moral lesson always keep a child interested and get him thinking. You could also try exposing a child to the precepts of all religions, and the commonality between them all. This will teach a child to question, accept and understand the universal brotherhood.

As a child, I remember my father getting Amar Chitra Kathas on the founders of all our religions—Buddha, Guru Nanak, Mohammed, Jesus—and on the mythology that makes Hinduism so fascinating. Through reading these when I was barely six or seven, I learnt that the kernel of all religions are intrinsically the same. This lesson has stayed with me all my life. Invest your time and effort in helping your child develop his or her mind. The payoff will be well worth it.

Key Takeaways

- Nourishing your child is a threefold process: nutrition for the body and emotional and mental stimulation for the mind.
- Be aware of how important family meal times are to set in place a lifetime of good dietary habits.
- Get your child involved in the process of preparing food.
- Focus on one on one interactions with your child.
- Stimulate his or her mind through interactions and books, as well as experiences.
- Minimise screen time; replace it with people, nature, and books.
- Encourage creativity. Make creative tasks part of your child's daily routine.
- Introduce your child to gratitude, empathy and tolerance, and through these introduce him to spirituality.
- Invest time and effort in nurturing your child's interests.

STEP FOUR: LOVE

The unconditional love a parent gives a child is the bulwark upon which the child's self-esteem is built.

Perhaps the expectation that a parent would love a child unconditionally is a given. It is also one of the toughest things one does as a parent. 'Children need love, especially when they do not deserve it,' said American psychiatrist Harold S. Hulbert. Kids are not always lovable, and any mom who has just scraped the remnants of her frayed patience off the floor of a supermarket aisle after her kid has just had the grandparent of all tantrums, would concur heartily. There have been times in my stint as a parent where I have understood why some animals eat their young. Kids can be tough, defiant, whiny pestilences put on this earth for the sole purpose of wearing down your sense of equanimity. Nonetheless, we love them unconditionally. It is a default factory setting for the maternal heart, and the paternal too, I assume. As author Ann Lamott wrote in her book, *Operating Instructions: A Journal of My Son's First Year*, 'I don't remember who said this, but there really are places in the heart you don't even know exist until you love a child.'

As a child, the one thing that kept me going every single day was the firm knowledge that no matter what happened, my mother (and of course, my father while he was alive) had my back. And that she loved me unconditionally. This knowledge was a warm blanket of security for me. And I hope the offspring has the same, though he has sorely tested this unconditionality at times. Author Nicholas Sparks said it well when he said, 'What it's like to be a parent: It's one of the hardest things you'll ever do but in exchange it teaches you the meaning of unconditional love.'

What is unconditional love between parent and child?

Unconditional love is when a child knows that no matter what he or she comes to you with, you will love him or her. Unconditional love is loving a child at all times: when the child has just made you proud by winning a championship trophy or topping his class or doing quite the reverse. You don't love the child on the basis of his or her behaviour or achievements—you love the child regardless. Says Mansi Zaveri, founder of kidsstoppress.com, one of the leading parenting websites in India, 'Parenting is the purest form of selfless love that you will ever experience. There is no perfect parent but every parent is the best parent their child could have.' There's an anecdote in American humourist Erma Bombeck's book, where she yells at her son in a supermarket, and the little chap in a flurry of tears looks all around and throws his arms around her for support. A child knows that beneath the anger and the yelling, the love is always there. As English journalist Jojo Moyes said, the child knows that 'Even if the whole world was throwing rocks at you, if you still had your mother or father at your back, you'd be okay. Some deep-rooted part of you would know you were loved. That you deserved to be loved.' The last line of that quote bears repetition; a child needs to know that he or she deserves to be loved. All the time.

Why do kids need unconditional love?

While children are sturdy little creatures, they're also very fragile. They are constantly finding themselves in a maze of peer relationships, judgmentalism and competitiveness. What they need is a space where they can truly be loved for themselves. We do love our kids without reservation, whether we admit it to ourselves or not. The author Roald Dahl wrote of this, in *Matilda*, when he said, 'It's a funny thing about mothers and fathers. Even when their own child is the most disgusting little blister you could ever imagine, they still think that he or she is wonderful.'

When I was a kid, I never quite fit in. I was overweight, geeky and thick-spectacled of the variant they called soda bottle. Every girl around me was growing into a wonderful swan, all long-limbed, smooth-skinned and gorgeous. I remained a squat, pimply-faced kid who wasn't cool enough to be part of the cool gang of girls at school. It bothered me a great deal. One day, when I returned home sobbing my heart out at being called 'fatso chasmiss', by one of the swans (yes, those were gentler times, the epithets my son and his friends hurl at each other these days could curdle milk), my mother simply gathered me and my shattered self-esteem to her and said, 'I love you, remember that.' I didn't realise how powerful those words were back then. And I repeat them to my son, when he returns from a spat at the playground or bristled at being ousted from a building cricket team for 'nofaultofmine' whining about 'No one wantstu be my fren.' 'I love you,' I tell him. Over and over again. And hope it soothes his hurt.

Demonstrate unconditional love over and over again

We've come a long way from the parenting precepts in the previous century where parents were encouraged to not hug and kiss their children for fear of spoiling them. It was Dr Benjamin Spock, with his book *Baby and Childcare* who rewrote the rules. He told new parents that their babies were people with minds of their own, and that parents should not hesitate to show them love and affection. As he famously said, and we must pay heed: 'Babies need love.'

Why is love important for a growing child and how does being loved impact a child's development?

You can blame biology for the rush of love that swamps you when you have your baby. The hormone oxytocin, also called the love hormone, is the key in moulding the requisite social behaviours which includes raising babies. This is essential because the human infant, as I mentioned earlier, does have a rather long period before he or she gets completely independent, unlike the offspring of most animals. Of course, the human infant might be physically independent much before he or she is booted out of the parental house into the big bad world, but the years as a baby have the maternal bloodstream awash with oxytocin rendering us hapless devoted slaves of these gurgling tyrants, who have us at their beck and call.

Babies form a bond with their mothers from within the uterus itself. In fact, according to some studies, a child's heart will begin to beat faster at the sound of his or her mother's voice because it recognises that voice from the uterus and it comforts him. For newborns, a soothing touch helps to calm them down, and apparently, this helps them develop their brain better because they sleep well as a result of being calmer. And it's not just newborns who benefit from skin on skin touch, new mothers too report lower levels of stress, and this makes them more sensitive to the baby's needs. It is also recommended that a baby be carried often so a mother can be more sensitive to its needs. Carrying a baby for at least three hours a day, and not just when the little one is bawling her head off, makes babies cry and fuss 51 per cent less, according to a McGill University research paper titled *Increased Carrying Reduces Infant Crying: A Randomized Controlled Trial* by Dr Urs Hunziker and Ronald Barr. For moms too, carrying a baby helps to produce more milk and reduce post-partum depression according to other research. An important benefit is that a child who is carried, rocked or played with (or even carried in a sling by a parent as they go around their day) gets enough vestibular stimulation to help develop visual alertness, tracking behaviour, motor and reflex development. A total win-win situation on the whole. So when you feel like holding your baby, snuggling up to him or her, breathing in the fresh baby smell, you know that you are bonding with your baby and you are helping your baby feel loved and wanted, and most importantly, secure, a need that will impact all their future relationship building and interaction with peers and others in the world as they grow.

How do you show your unconditional love to your child?

I remember a particularly bad midterm exam when I was in the sixth grade. I was terrified of showing my grades to my mother, and didn't inform her about the date of the Parent-Teacher Meeting (PTM). I underestimated the power of the school gate mom tribe, and this was decades before the infernal school mom WhatsApp groups. To my complete shock and consternation, I saw my mother walk into my class, when my roll number was called out. Not by a word or a gesture did she give away that I had not informed her about the PTM. I got hauled over the coals for it when I reached home that day, but in public, in front of the class and the teacher, she was supportive and loving. And I knew then, as I know today, that no matter how annoyed or angry my mom is with me, she will never ever show her displeasure in public. My mom has my back, and that is my security blanket always. Or as I read recently, she will always be my querencia, which is a lovely Spanish term for a place where a person feels the most comforted.

The world's greatest boxing legend, Muhammad Ali, speaks of the confidence his mother gave him when he was finding it difficult to study, given his dyslexia. To quote from his book, *The Soul of a Butterfly*, 'My mother once told me that my confidence in myself made her believe in me. I thought that was funny, because it was her confidence in me that strengthened my belief in myself. I didn't realise it then, but from the very beginning, my parents were helping me build the foundation for my life.'

Hollywood superstar Ryan Gosling was bullied terribly when he was at school and had trouble reading too. To top his woes, he was also diagnosed as having Attention-deficit Hyperactivity Disorder (ADHD) and didn't have any friends until he was a teenager. His mother took a year off and homeschooled him. He began his acting career after that, and never looked back. When he was nominated for an Oscar in 2006, he said, 'It meant a lot to me because it meant a lot to the people I love, especially my mother. She's been fighting for me since I was born.'

How do we let our children know they're loved?

I am a very demonstrative mom, embarrassingly so for the offspring, because I heap the kisses and hugs, unmindful at times that he is now a cool teen, and therefore too grown up to be the recipient of the same. My mother wasn't very demonstrative but the love was just the same, if not more. As American novelist Pearl S. Buck wisely put it, 'Some mothers are kissing mothers and some are scolding mothers, but it is love just the same, and most mothers kiss and scold together.' The offspring possibly concurs with the last bit of the sentence, given that he's awarded me the title of 'Meanest Mom in the World'.

But we are all different in the way we show our love to our kids. Some of us are overtly demonstrative, and hug and kiss our kids as much as we can. Some of us are not, and we cannot compel ourselves to be demonstrative parents. Which does not in any way mean that we love our children any less. Being demonstrative though, is not the only way one can show one's love to one's children. Love is shown in all our interactions with them, when we take pride in them, in not just their achievements, but also their efforts. Love is accepting them in the here and now and being proud of what they are, and telling them that they are good enough, and encouraging them to do better than they think they can.

Different ways of demonstrating unconditional love

- **Forgiveness:** Forgive your child for mistakes, bad behaviour and back talk. Do let your child know that the behaviour is not acceptable, but forgive it. Let your child know that you love them, and you have forgiven them but you expect them to correct the behaviour.
- **Reassurance:** Tell your child you love them every single day. As often as you want. As often as you can. Hug them. Kiss them. As Diana, Princess of Wales, said, 'Hugs can do great amounts of good, especially for children.'

- **Talk Positive:** Tell them you believe in them, in what you think they are capable of and beyond, and that you see them achieving what they set out to achieve. Word your feedback positively, focus on the outcome.

Be a sensitive caregiver

Along with unconditional love, your child needs sensitive caregiving. As the term itself suggests, sensitive caregiving is when children are responded to and know they are loved. A 2014 study conducted on people who came from poor families found that the children who received 'sensitive caregiving' from birth to age three were the ones who went on to fare better academically and were able to have better interpersonal relationships when they grew up. According to a report in *psychcentral.com*, 'Emerging research discovers sensitive caregiving in the first three years of life is a strong predictor of an individual's future social competence and academic success.' Adds the report, 'Sensitive caregiving is defined as the extent to which a parent responds to a child's signals appropriately and promptly, is positively involved during interactions with the child, and provides a secure base for the child's exploration of the environment.'

Is there a fallout if a child does not receive sensitive caregiving in the early years? According to the *Scientific American*, 'Many children who have not had ample physical and emotional attention are at higher risk for behavioural, emotional and social problems as they grow up.' Therefore, paying attention to your infant, talking to them, even in baby talk, responding to cries and calls, interacting with them, hugging them and kissing them, all play a vital role in reinforcing a child's sense of security and self-esteem, which will in turn stand the child in good stead when he or she has to deal with the world.

Sensitive caregiving also lets a child get attached to the mother or primary caregiver, which in turn lets a child explore the world with the security of being watched and taken care of. There's research to support it. Children need presence and attention. Research conducted by Harry Harlow on baby monkeys showed that they clung grimly onto dummy cloth monkeys when separated from their mothers. With children, if mothers or the primary caregiver are not mirroring or paying attention to their cues, or being affectionate with them, they could be setting the stage for a lifetime of self-esteem, relationship, trust and other issues which will fund some therapist's vacation home. We must listen to researcher Dr Brene Brown when she says, 'The real questions for parents should be: Are you engaged? Are you paying attention?' This is the biggest gift we could give our kids: being engaged in their lives and paying attention.

Why is sensitive caregiving so important?

Research was conducted amongst children from orphanages, who were deprived of sensitive caregiving and touch in their formative years. Here's what they found.

To quote from a study published in *Development and Psychopathology*, 'Below the surface, some children from deprived surroundings such as orphanages, have vastly different hormone levels than their parent-raised peers even beyond the baby years. For instance, in Romania in the 1980s, by ages six to twelve, levels of the stress hormone cortisol were still much higher in children who had lived in orphanages for more than eight months than in those who were adopted at or before the age of four months.' Other studies show that children who did not receive adequate touch and caregiving during the early years had different levels of oxytocin and vasopressin (hormones that have been linked to emotion and social bonding), despite having had an average of three years in a family home. The environment change into a loving and caregiving home did not override the deprived early years.

> **KEY TAKEAWAYS**
>
> - Do not hold back on the love you show your child, by word or gesture. These are deposits you make into the repository that is your child's future, and play a vital role in helping your child build his or her self confidence as they grow into adults.
>
> - Be the comfort that your child can turn to as often as they wish.
>
> - Hug and kiss your child as often as you can.
>
> - Be a sensitive caregiver.

STEP FIVE: INSPIRE

You are your child's first role model.
Be one he or she can look up to.

We are not perfect. In fact, we are far from it. The perfect parent does not exist, or if it does, it is cloaked in the mythical realm of fiction. Atticus Finch of *To Kill a Mockingbird*, Marmee of *Little Women*, the Weasleys of the *Harry Potter* series, for instance. But for the little humans we have created, we are emblematic of all that adulthood represents. To them we are their role models, for better or for worse. They look to us for cues as to how to behave, how to handle the world. They may not do what we tell them to do, but they're watching what we do very carefully. To quote from Dr Brene Brown's *Daring Greatly: How the Courage to be Vulnerable Transforms the Way We Live, Love, Parent and Lead*, 'Who we are and how we engage with the world are much stronger predictors of how our children will do than what we know about parenting. Are you the adult that you want your child to grow up to be?'

Bringing up a child is making sure you're living your life in a fishbowl because everything you do is being watched with a pair of curious eyes and listened to with rabbit ears. That four-letter word that unwittingly slipped out when you almost rear ended another car in a bad traffic moment? Your two year old has filed it carefully in his brain and will bring it up at the most inopportune public moment, preferably a time when you have elderly relatives around to purse their lips disapprovingly at this evidence of your lack of parenting skills. Pay heed to Italian physician and educator Maria Montessori's words when she says, 'A child is an eager observer and is particularly attracted by the actions of the adults and wants to imitate them.' So bite back that epithet before it spills out, and know that you are being watched and you will be imitated.

The other role models of the superlative variety, like Superman, Batman, Percy Jackson, Harry Potter, Sachin Tendulkar or Virat Kohli will come later.

The offspring, a rapscallion at the best times, is one who is always particular about certain things. Simple things. He will always change into his nightclothes before bedtime and brush his teeth. The other day, we had a houseguest who remarked how wonderful it was that he did it without being reminded. 'I guess, that's because he's seen you doing it every night,' my guest added. It struck me then, that when the child does imitate the little things, it should be natural for him to imitate the bigger things, so my fingers, toes and eyes are crossed that he does the same with the other more important things that really matter. There was a kernel of truth in what the author Robert Fulghum said, 'Don't worry that children never listen to you; worry that they are always watching you.'

Think about it. More often than not we tell our kids not to lie no matter what the compulsion. But then at the same time we don't hesitate to tell them to say we are not at home when someone we don't want to interact with rings the doorbell. We often tell them little white lies all the time. When they realise they've been lied to, what breaks is not only their trust but also their belief in us as parents as unimpeachable. As someone wise and anonymous said, 'Children seldom misquote. In fact, they usually repeat word for word what you shouldn't have said.'

Apart from imitating behaviour, children also consciously and unconsciously imbibe attitudes, thought processes and mindsets from us parents. I realised it when my son, would, without fail, thank the liftman when we reached our floor. I didn't need to tell him to do so, he would see me doing so, and just fell into the habit of imitating me. Unfortunately, he doesn't seem to have taken after me in the speaking softly, for he can make an unwary eardrum ring when in full voice, but then that is probably an unconscious imitation of the Y chromosome.

It isn't just tangible behaviours that children imitate; it is also the value systems that we show them that they model their own on. Bill Gates, the co-founder of Microsoft in an interview with GeekWire, spoke about how his father had been a role model for him. His father, he said, helped him develop his sense of justice, fair play, prudence and business sense.

Here's a touching story about a father and son, Dick Hoyt, and his son Rick Hoyt. Together they go by the name Team Hoyt, an athletic team that competes triathlons. What is unusual about this team, you would think? Here's why. The son, Rick was born with cerebral palsy, caused by the umbilical cord twisting around his neck, blocking the flow of oxygen. The Hoyts were told by doctors that they would have to institutionalise Rick who, they said, would be 'nothing more than a vegetable'. What gave the Hoyts hope was that Rick's eyes would follow them around the room, and the parents began, with the help of the doctors at the Children's Hospital in Boston, treating Rick like any other child. With persistence, he learned the alphabet, then was fitted with a computer that helped him communicate, went on to attend school and graduate from Boston University. Team Hoyt was formed in 1977, when Rick wanted to run in a race to benefit a lacrosse player from his school who was paralysed. At that point, Dick was thirty-six years old and not a runner. But father and son completed the race together, with Dick pushing Rick's wheelchair. After the first race, Rick told his father, that when he ran, he didn't feel he was handicapped. It was this statement which spurred Dick to begin training to run every day—with a bag of cement in a wheelchair. By March 2016, Team Hoyt had competed in seventy-two marathons and seven triathlons. If that isn't a parent who walks, runs and swims the talk, I don't know what is.

So, how do we become parents who walk the talk?

The Macedonian prince, Alexander III, the son of Philip II, was born to a king who ruled over a small Hellenic state in ancient Greece. He spent his early years seeing his father transform Macedonia into a great military power. Was it any wonder then, that when Alexander inherited the throne at the age of twenty, he set about building on his father's legacy and expanded his empire so magnificently, creating one of the largest empires in that era, from Greece all the way to north-western India.

Children take what they learn from their parents, whether to conquer and rule, or whether to take joy in their everyday work. Children not only listen to what you say, they also watch what you do. If you think nothing of littering the street, parking in no-parking zones, breaking red lights, talking on the phone while driving, your child grows up thinking these implicit civic rules are not meant to be taken seriously. There are small rules we all break every day, without even realising them, but our kids pick this up. The comedian, activist and author George Carlin has words of wisdom we should pay heed to. He says, 'If your kid needs a role model and you ain't it, you're both f**ked.'

Here's what you need to do to walk the talk:

- **Be truthful**: Most children are born honest, and are honest even when it is embarrassing for them to be so. When a child knows that his parent will always tell the truth no matter what, it is an example for him to follow.

- **Be polite**: Teaching a child to be polite is very often show and tell. A child will echo what he or she sees, so if you, the first role model he or she sees, doesn't speak politely that might become their default setting. If you talk with a raised voice all the time, your child might think that is the norm. So along with your listening ears, be also aware of your talking voice, when you're interacting with your kids, or with others around in their presence.

- **Apologise**: Don't be afraid of the 'S' word. Saying sorry comes all too difficult for us, but when children see that we aren't able to apologise when we are in the wrong, it makes them believe that apologising is a sign of weakness and giving in. If you have been in a situation where you have been in the wrong, and the child has been right, don't be afraid to apologise. By doing so you are only teaching your child that it is quite alright to own up to one's mistakes, and convert this into a life lesson.

- **Abide by civic rules**: From the little things like littering and breaking queues, to larger things like bribing your way through traffic violations and taking bribes to get things done, children notice everything you do. You lose the moral authority to speak to them about right and wrong if they've seen you doing what is considered wrong.

- **Encourage positive behaviour:** We all know the story of the young George Washington, who after having hacked down a hapless cherry tree, confessed to the crime when asked with the charming disclaimer, that he could not tell a lie. His father, instead of doing the regular thing, and biting the little chappie's ear off, was delighted by his son's honesty, and said it was 'worth more than a thousand trees'.

- **Broaden your horizons:** Unless you as a parent are open to learning about the world around you, how would you expose your child to the same. The Nobel Laureate Rabindranath Tagore came from a family renowned for its influence over Bengali culture and literature. As a consequence, Tagore was introduced to theatre, music, art and literature at a very early age. A turning point in his life was, when he was barely eleven, his father took him on tour across India which exposed him to the multifaceted beauty that the country had. He also read a lot on this journey. On his return from this trip, the dams of creativity which had been swelling within him since his childhood, were opened, and he composed a long poem in the Maithili style. Giving the child an environment that facilitates curiosity and creativity is essential to encourage learning.

- **Embody the values:** Do what you want your child to learn to do. English businessman Richard Branson speaks about his mother, who was always focused on thinking up ways to make money. They had no television in the house, and Eve Branson would spend a lot of her time in their shed, making tissue boxes and waste papers bins that she sold to stores, including the famous store, Harrods. Her husband, Richard's father, Ted, created pressing devices that would hold the boxes together to be glued. The entire project became a proper cottage industry. Branson learnt the value of initiative early, and that of enterprise. He also learnt the invaluable lesson of learning quickly from failure and moving on swiftly to the next initiative. No management school could have taught him this so efficiently, and today we know Richard Branson for his brand Virgin, which encompasses everything from music to entertainment to airlines, and now space travel. That his parents were living examples of innovation and entrepreneurship to no small extent contributed to Branson's penchant for nimble entrepreneurship.

Creating the right environment for the child to learn life lessons from is vital. To quote Canadian journalist and author, Malcolm Gladwell, 'The conventional explanation for Jewish success, of course, is that Jews come from a literate, intellectual culture. They are famously "the people of the book." There is surely something to that. But it wasn't just the children of rabbis who went to law school. It was the children of garment workers. And their critical advantage in climbing the professional ladder wasn't the intellectual rigour you get from studying the Talmud. It was the practical intelligence and savvy you get from watching your father sell aprons on Hester Street.'

My mother worked in a bank all her working life. Come rain or shine, or ill-health, I remember mom draping her crisply starched saree efficiently, picking up her handbag and heading out to work. It is something I have internalised, without her ever needing to tell me so. No matter how you feel, get up, dress up and show up. This lesson is something I hope the offspring learns from me. And then, it always works both ways, doesn't it! To be an inspiring parent, you must push yourself to be an inspiring person. As Haim Ginott, child psychologist stated, 'Children are like wet cement whatever falls on them makes an impression.' It would do us well to ensure that all that falls on to our children, makes an impression that is pleasant and beneficial.

Key Takeaways

- Be a parent who walks the talk.
- Children unconsciously imbibe from their parents, habits, gestures, behaviours.
- You need to set the norms for the behaviour you would like to see from your child.
- Whether it is being polite, eating healthy or being active, know that you are the role model your child is looking up to.

STEP SIX: CHALLENGE

A child can only stretch beyond his capabilities when challenged.

When my son was very young, he had a terror of water so strident that even getting him to wash his hair was an exercise that made my hair bleach itself white from the roots. Getting him to wet his feet in the sea was the stuff of nightmares. Swimming? Ha. Perish the thought. We spent our very first vacation in Goa with him, having him stand by the safety of a distantly beached boat yelling out for his father to return from the sea or risk being 'died'.

He would never learn to swim, I thought, resigning myself to visions of him being the only one at college frat pool parties with a tube around him and floaters on his arms. Or so I thought. The spouse was made of sterner stuff. On one vacation at a hotel with a pool, he took himself into the pool. The offspring sat at the side, delicately dipping his toes into the chlorinated water, admonishing his father at repeated intervals to not go too deep or he would be 'drownded and died'. Such grim thoughts apart, the spouse slowly pulled him into the shallow end and made him stand in the water.

He was engrossed in playing ball when the spouse managed to entice him further into the deep, until the water was almost neck deep. And then he threw the ball just a tad out of his reach. The offspring didn't even realise when he struck out—wading, floundering and splashing—to reach the ball, the air tyre around his waist making him buoyant. Within seconds he was navigating his way around the pool, chortling away manically, under the eagle-eyed supervision of his father who kept pushing the ball away from him. It took him another summer to learn how to swim. Eventually, he trained as a competitive swimmer and reached state levels in a couple of years. It was a long journey from a child who could not bear to have his head underwater.

Perhaps the greatest power in the universe is the thrill of being able to master a skill, whether it is simply your baby being able to flip herself from her back to her belly, or your ten-year-old perfecting a complicated tune on the keyboard. Every child comes ready fitted with immense creative potential. Within each child is hidden a potential artist, mathematical genius, inventor, dancer, musician and it is up to us, their parents, to spot the latent talent and encourage the child to reach beyond what they believe themselves capable of.

Take the great composer Wolfgang Amadeus Mozart, for example. When he was barely four, his father taught him a few minuets which he played with ease and soon he was composing small pieces of music by the age of five. In fact, his father was the only teacher Mozart had as a child. He was keen to learn and often surprised his father with his talent. His father taught him not only music but also languages.

Educators advise letting the child drive the learning. As early childhood educationist Maria Montessori wisely said, 'Never help a child with a task at which he feels he can succeed.' Malcolm Gladwell put forth the theory that to excel at a particular skill, what is needed is 10,000 hours of practice to excel at the skill. In his book, Gladwell says, 'Practice isn't the thing you do once you're good. It's the thing you do that makes you good.' According to researchers, the children who go on to achieve things, are not necessarily the ones who are born with talent, but the ones who have the grit to stick to the practise of the skill even when the odds are against them. Cultivating grit, or the ability to stick with the task, is important if you want your child to excel at the talent that he or she has been given.

Here's where you come in. You must make note when something completely captivates your child, and no, we're not talking Doraemon here. If you find your child is happiest slamming a ball around on a tennis court, enrol him in professional coaching. If your child spends hours sketching and painting, bring him books on art and materials to keep sketching and painting. You will know when a child has found what interests him or her.

Sometimes, what leads to certain insights might seem completely unrelated to the field, so you never know what might impact a child in what way in the future. Albert Einstein, for example, states his famous theory of relativity came to him through intuition, and this intuition was made strong through music. While his mother had enrolled him in music lessons at the tender age of five his love for music actually developed much later when he was a teenager. He began teaching himself music after he fell in love with Mozart's sonatas. He said about his rediscovered love for music, 'Love is a better teacher than a sense of duty.'

Feed the passion

If you recognise a latent passion, a spark of interest and talent in your child, you must feed that passion. The example of the unsung sport parent requires a special mention here. Saina Nehwal has often spoken about how her father would take her every single morning to train at 4.30 a.m. and wait patiently until she'd finished her training. Chess maestro Vishwanathan Anand learnt the basics of chess from his mother, Sushila when he was very young. On realising he had the talent and the interest, Sushila did all within her means to ensure he received the requisite training and opportunities to play. To quote her from one of her rare interviews, 'I don't want to say that I was behind his achievement. A mother has to be by the side of the child taking baby steps in any field. In my case, it happened to be chess.'

Olympic swimmer Nathan Adrian's parents reported driving 100,000 miles in four years, taking vacations in fifteen different cities in the US, and probably clocking 100,000 air miles. According to Jim Adrian, Nathan Adrian's father, in an interview, 'It wasn't cheap, but it was worth it. It's a good investment. You always invest in your kids.'

Be realistic

Getting the job done is important and you can relax your standards about perfection as long as the child is enjoying it. As parents we all want to keep upping the bar for our kids, but if the bar is too high beyond the capabilities of the child, he or she might lose all interest. Think about it, if someone came to you and offered you a couple of lakhs or even a few crores to do a pole vault like Dipa Karmakar attempted, would you agree. You wouldn't, no matter how much the temptation because you aren't trained and know you aren't capable of doing it, and might seriously injure yourself. Similarly with a child, tempting a child with rewards on achievements which are not possible at his or her level of development, just sets the stage for disappointment. Rewards and punishments won't work if basic capability is not present.

Pushing a child to achieve will be counterproductive if the goal is much beyond the child's capacity. Ideally, you must set the level of achievement at just a little beyond your child's capability and keep increasing it incrementally. This challenges and motivates the child and allows for the development of internal motivation if they believe they are capable of achieving the goals set. If a child is constantly unable to achieve very high goals, he or she will believe that it is beyond their capacity and stop making the effort.

Psychologist Mihalyi Csikszentmihalyi from the University of Chicago put forth a simple theory which says that if a child will lose interest in a task in two situations: one, if he is above the challenge level of a task; or two, if he is not up to the challenge level of the task. The outcome is the same in both instances. Earl Woods, father of golf legend Tiger Woods, introduced his son to golf when he was barely two. By the time he was eleven, Tiger had beaten his father. Interestingly, neither Earl nor his wife Tilda were over-involved parents in Tiger's golfing career. They did facilitate it to the best of their ability, even coached him in his early years, but the motivation came entirely from Tiger himself. Self-motivation is the best motivation. But only, and do make a note of this, if the inherent capability is there.

When the offspring was in the swimming circuit, there was a young boy who joined their batch a few months after the batch had begun. While he was fairly efficient at the stroke, he unfortunately lagged far behind the other kids in his group and within a couple of months he stopped coming to the pool to train. The parent had enrolled him into the academy because they thought he was good at swimming, but unfortunately, they hadn't done a realistic assessment of the other swimmers his age he would be up against. Unable to keep pace with the better swimmers, he lost interest and stopped swimming completely, which was a pity because he could have been good had he persisted.

Recognise the possibilities within your child, but don't overlay them with your own thwarted ambition. How you react when your child performs poorly because the level is too high may affect whether he is affected negatively by the experience. You risk blaming him for failure. This might even lead you to believe that your child is incapable, and through your words and behaviour, transmit this unjustified belief to him. This, on a consistent basis, can undermine a child's self-esteem which will affect them in all aspects of their life.

Encourage creative play

It may seem like something purposeless to our adult eyes but play is perhaps the greatest tool to help your child learn. Play-based learning is a very important educational and psychological concept to help kids make sense of their world and understand concepts. Through play, a child develops not just social skills in order to play with other kids, but also matures, gains self confidence to take on new challenges, and develops cognitive thinking. A child with a box, making it a television set, or a pile of wooden blocks creating a tower is using a most precious commodity, namely his imagination and creativity, to reflect his experience.

To quote Roger Van Oech, author and toy maker who focused on the study of creativity, 'Necessity may be the mother of invention, but play is certainly the father.' Another person who knew something about the importance of creative play was development psychologist Jean Piaget, who said 'Play is the work of childhood.' He knew a bit about this, being a development psychologist who put forth the theory about the nature and development of human intelligence. It isn't just human children who play. All mammals play as children. Through play they learn the skills they need to draw on when they are adults—from socialising to finding food.

In the book *Einstein Never Used Flash Cards*, five important elements of play are listed, namely:

- It must be enjoyable and give a child pleasure.
- It should have no extrinsic goals, and no prescribed learning.
- It should be voluntary and spontaneous.
- The player should be actively engaged in play.
- And there must be an element of make-believe in the play.

Another advantage to creative play is that it allows children to rehearse potential scenarios in their mind and respond appropriately in a non threatening manner. Also, play is controlled risk taking for children. Be the parent who encourages mistakes, spills, drawing on the walls (providing off course, the wall paint is wipe off, let's be practical here) and allows table cloths to be cut up in the interest of costumes for plays being staged by your dramatic genius in the making. To quote Bruce Nussbaum, professor of innovation and design, from his book *Creative Intelligence*, 'When people are playing, they take risks they would not ordinarily take. They experience failure not as a crushing blow but as an idea they tried that didn't work. Play transforms problems into challenges, seriousness into fun, one right answer into any number of possible outcomes.'

The very definition of creativity is getting redefined with every generation. Who would have thought twenty years ago that creativity wouldn't necessarily be about creating art but about creating apps? We need to prepare our children for the creativity that jobs we don't even know about in the future will demand from them, and that requires them to keep their mental muscles flexed and in ship shape. How does play help in creative problem solving, you wonder?

Building sandcastles or a fort with sheets and sticks for instance, sets into place principles of space, dimensions and construction; play-acting and role-playing help in creative thinking and the development of the imagination. A child who writes out a play, creates costumes and a set, and sells tickets to his show has already begun on the basics of honing his creativity, delved into fashion and set design, and this play could be his initial foray into entrepreneurship. The lessons learnt from these childhood escapades always stand a child in good stead, they learn from play what no amount of formal lessons could possibly teach them, primarily because these are self driven, and make them think, rationalise, come to their own conclusions and draw up solutions to the problems they experience by themselves. Also, a child who sits in a cardboard carton pretending it is a car, knows it is a carton. To him, the carton is as much a toy car as a carton, and perhaps he can flip it over and make it a fort. Assimilating and accommodating all these realities makes for creative flexibility and develops creative thinking. Various researchers including J.L. Dansky, C. Hutt, R. Bhavani and J. Johnson have determined that object play helps with developing divergent problem solving skills, as does make believe or fantasy play.

Most children are intensely energetic and physical. Physical play allows them the opportunity to release their pent-up energy, and discharge the stress hormones that would otherwise lead them into tantrums. Playing with your child also helps you get closer to your child and bond. There's also a hidden benefit to play. According to John Ratey, author of the book *Spark: The Revolutionary New Science of Exercise and the Brain*, just ten minutes of physical activity can change the way the brain functions, and makes you feel better.

An interesting finding from a survey by IBM which spoke with 1,500 CEOs found that they considered creativity as the most valuable resource they sought in managers. According to research conducted by Jonathan Plucker, a professor of educational psychology at the University of Connecticut, creativity tests given to high school children were thrice as effective as IQ tests in predicting adult achievement. And what sparks a creative bent of mind? You guessed it—play!

Here are some easy ways to encourage play and challenge your child's mind:

- Read books to them, and encourage them to read books.
- Get them into the habit of solving puzzles.
- Interest them in making science projects with you. It makes them think about how things work, and think out of the box. It also teaches them to question things and arrive at their own conclusions with empirical evidence.
- Teaching them maths early is important. Beginning school with a rudimentary knowledge of numbers and

mathematical concepts helps future achievements in mathematics.
- Encourage creative play. Give the time and tools to hone their creativity through play.

Be the parent who pushes enough

Seeing how modern kids are overscheduled to a minute, with school, extracurricular classes, tuitions and more, it would seem that parents have gone from beyond being merely pushy, to being so pushy that the kids might just reach escape velocity. Sometimes, given peer pressure, the kids themselves are keen to do a lot of extracurricular activities in order not to feel left behind. At times, as a parent, one often wonders if one is being too pushy and the child might grow up with a serious sense of resentment towards one for ruining what should have been an idyllic chilled out childhood. However, research published in the *Journal of the Society for Research in Child Development* suggests that children who are introduced to a wide range of activities in early childhood benefit from it later in life. According to Joseph Mahoney, associate professor of psychology at Yale and the lead author of this research, 'Our research shows that children who take part in organised activities benefit developmentally. They are healthier, judging from their academic performance and indicators of psychological and emotional wellbeing and self-esteem, as well as from their use of cigarettes, alcohol and drugs, and their parent-child relationships.'

Ideally though, it should be the child driving the pushing, the child wanting to set her own goals, with the parent providing the bulwark of support and the occasional prod between the shoulder blades to get back on track. Pushing a child who doesn't want to do something, even if you think he has talent can often bring misery and resentment, and be rather counter productive.

Easier said than done, but be the parent who pushes enough. I'm guilty of being on the other extreme I confess, the parent who doesn't push at all, with the result that the offspring has grown up like a weed. In retrospect though, I realise that a steady, gentle push would have stood him, and me too, in good stead. Sometimes, though, it isn't about the overt push. It could perhaps just believe the quiet, steady belief that the child will do well for himself.

Ariana Huffington, the founder of huffingtonpost.com says, 'I was brought up in a one bedroom apartment in Athens, Greece. (My mother) made me feel that I could aim for the stars. And if I failed along the way, that is okay. Failure is not the opposite of success, she used to say, it's a stepping stone to success.' And of course, there's the Pygmalion effect, which states 'that what one person expects of another can come to serve as a self-fulfilling prophecy.' With kids, your expectations are the spring board from which they leap out into the world.

KEY TAKEAWAYS

- Recognise potential, create the right environment and give opportunity for the child to maximise her interest and potential.

- Challenge your child, push her out of her comfort zone, but don't push so hard that the child loses the enjoyment for the task.

- As a parent, set higher goals and standards for your child and be the support to help him or her reach there.

- Walk the delicate balance between being pushy and being someone who challenges a child to extend him or herself.

STEP SEVEN: CONNECT

*Not only animals but also ancient human cultures formed cooperative groups to raise their children.
Thus, there is truth in the African proverb, 'It takes a village to raise a child.'*

It is said that the quickest way for a parent to get a child's attention is to sit down and look comfortable. A small confession here. When the offspring was born, I wouldn't have survived the initial few months without my mother and my mother-in-law stepping in and showing me how things are done. Right from the basics like holding a newborn, to feeding the little bundle who terrorised me with his feed, poop and change routine that seemed to go on till my eyelids needed to be propped open with toothpicks, I needed to learn every single thing. The lady who came in to massage and bathe him made me more confident about handling him on my own, given I was terrified I would do something wrong since he was so tiny and squirmy, as babies are. I had heard terrible stories about what happened to babies who had been dropped on their heads, and I was all the more nervous in my handling of him. My sis-in-law, her baby being a strapping tween, showed me patiently how to swaddle the offspring so he could sleep soundly, comforted by the restriction reminiscent of the womb. My paediatrician calmly sat through my panic-stricken visits when I was convinced the offspring was headed for some terrible illness and reassured me that it was nothing that some paracetamol drops couldn't fix.

His aunts and uncle pampered him silly, his cousins played with him and indulged him till he seriously began to believe the sun, moon and stars shone out of his rear, a notion that thankfully going to big school quickly disabused him of. Over the years, the offspring's circle of influence has expanded from the immediate family to the playschool, then the big school, from a single class teacher to multiple subject teachers and tuition teachers, from his father teaching him how to kick his way to swim and coaches working with him refining his stroke. Now the WhatsApp school mommy group is my 24/7 lifeline as we negotiate the precarious territory of high school.

I could have never raised him on my own. Forget humans, even animals know that raising a child is not a single-handed effort. Elephants roaming the Savannah bring up babies in a group of related females. That means a baby elephant grows up with his mom, his aunts, his cousin-sisters all around to keep an eagle eye on him and smack him with their trunks if he gets out of line. The group is led by a matriarch who keeps order. When there is danger, the female elephants form a circle looking outwards, keeping the elephant calves within and thus safe from predators. Sometimes, female elephants from other herds kidnap a calf, in which case, the entire herd gets together in order to get the baby back.

Giraffes, too, have their version of a nursery, called a calving pool, where a mommy giraffe can leave her baby and go off to forage for food, knowing that her baby is safe until her return and will be watched over by another mamma. On the Galapagos islands, sea lions have their own parenting system. Groups of moms, some with toddlers, give birth on a beach guarded by a single male sea lion. Some may be part of his harem, some may not. This nursery has a baby pool of sorts, where mamma sea lions can drop off their week-old infants to play with other sea lion pups while other females keep watch by rotation. In truth, it does take *a village to raise a child*. Bringing up a child is a task that is a team effort and needs to be shared with the larger family and society.

Anthropologist Karen Kramer of the University of Utah, along with her colleagues, created an economic hypothesis regarding this. She says, 'We simulated an economic problem that would have arisen over the course of human evolution. As mothers became more successful at producing children, they also had more dependents than they could care for on their own. We found that early in that transition, it was a mother's older children who helped to raise her younger children and only with more modern life histories did mothers also need the cooperation of other adults. This suggests that early human families may have formed around cooperating groups of mothers and children.'

Anthropologist and primatologist Sarah Hardy writes in *Mothers and Others: The Evolutionary Origins of Mutual Understanding* that human babies have always needed not just their mothers but support from an entire tribe of siblings, father, aunts, grandparents, relatives and friends. She theorises that communal child care amongst humans dates back to the Pleistocene era, it being essential for human infants to survive in conditions of food scarcity and dangerous predators.

Malcolm Gladwell speaks about children who had the potential to make it big in life, the intelligence or the talent required for success, but ended up not making it. He says, 'They lacked something that could have been given to them if we'd only known they needed it: a community around them that prepared them properly for the world.'

In early communities, the extended family and the neighbourhood wholeheartedly participated in the raising of a child. In certain cultures—Indian, Eastern, Latino, for example—grandparents and extended family have always been a part of a child's life. According to a paper published in the June 2007 edition of *Clinical Child and Family Psychology Review*, cultures influenced by collectivist and communal concepts are more likely to embrace the extended family model. In fact, in African, Middle Eastern, Asian and Latin cultures, most families operate as a whole, in terms of finance, business and property. It is but natural then, that child-rearing also is a joint effort.

In China, an infant is believed to have arrived from the gods with inherent goodness. The elders are considered responsible for training, educating, disciplining and imparting values to a child according to the Confucian wisdom. Interestingly, according to the Shanghai Municipal Population and Family Planning Commission, around 90 per cent of the younger children in the city are cared for by grandparents, and these grandparents provide most often exclusive care of the grandchild while the parents work. In Chinese society, the retirement age is sixty, and they do have a tradition of living in multigenerational families, not very different from the joint family system we have in India.

In India we are very strong on the extended family being participatory in the lives of the children. While most families are slowly segueing into the nuclear in urban areas, we still remain closely connected to the extended family. Religious festivals, weddings and birthdays are celebrated traditionally with the extended family. Many communities are very close-knit and have regular meetings so that members can mingle and the younger generation can learn about their antecedents. Communal parenting has benefits that go beyond mere convenience. All adults in the immediate neighbourhood or community feel some degree of responsibility for every child they come in contact with. Also, seeing examples within the community helps a child learn quicker.

Surprisingly, even in the western world, the dependence on the wider network seems to be growing. According to the American Association of Retired Persons, 4.5 million children under the age of eighteen are growing up in grandparent-headed households, and in one-third of these homes no parent is present. This figure has increased 30 percent since 1990 and the ethnicity crosses all lines. Given that senior citizens today have better health and longer life expectancy, they are around longer and in reasonably good health to participate in the raising of the grandchildren. The comedian Rita Rudner was probably joking when she said, 'Have children while your parents are still young enough to take care of them,' but there is something that rings true in that statement.

Being raised in an extended communal network of family and friends is advantageous for a child as well. A study in Australia found that children from three to nineteen months had higher learning scores when cared for by extended family in addition to their parents. Having an entire village raise a child helps in making a child a social being, given that man is a social animal and as the wise poet John Donne said, *'No man is an island.'*

Given than modern living very often is of nuclear families, transferable jobs and moving away from the gambit of immediate families, friends and community come to play a vital role in the raising of a child. When your friends come visiting, or when you spend time with your friends, your child also does so. The discussions, the conversations, the influences a child gathers at this time can be immensely important in building up who he or she will eventually be. Very often, a child might form a bond with one of your friends that makes it easier for her to discuss issues that are bothering her without worrying about how you might react to it. Also, the friends you have offer your child a glimpse into the adult world which might differ from how they see you.

Veteran actress Shabana Azmi grew up in the charged atmosphere of her home which had her parents'—poet Kaifi Azmi and mother Shaukat Azmi's friends visiting often. At an event, she stated how the atmosphere she grew up in influenced her social activism. She stated that the political discussions with all her parents' friends at home were where she got all her political information from, as well as her passion towards working for those lesser privileged. This social consciousness eventually reflected itself in the kinds of films and roles she chose, as well as the social causes she put her heft behind as a celebrity with a voice that would be heard, most notably, the Nivara Haq Samiti where she joined up with film maker Anand Patwardhan to fight for the rights of slum dwellers in Mumbai. Children need to have other adults they can trust and rely on, and here's where your friends step in. They form the second line of influence after both parents and the immediate family. And these influences can have an immense impact on them.

What are the advantages of raising a child as part of an extended community?

- **Ethnic identity:** A great deal of development of ethnic identity comes from listening to stories from the older people in the family and taking part in family traditions and functions. The telling and retelling of stories, the narratives whether mythological, fictional or even personal, all promote cultural continuity in the next generation. This sense of cultural belonging can help build a healthy self-esteem.

- **Intermediates in parent-child conflict:** When there is an extended family or a tightly-knit community, tense situations between parents and children can be resolved by intervention by an older member of the family like a grandparent or a neighbour. Interestingly, in traditional African and Latino cultures children can go live with other members of the extended family until the enraged parent calms down. An American television host used to joke that 'the reason grandchildren and grandparents get along so well is that they have a common enemy.'

- **Back-up:** A closely knit community also serves as a back-up in case of a major life changing event like the death of a parent, a divorce, bankruptcy or a major illness. The neighbourhood or the extended community steps in to care for a child if a parent is not able to for any reason.

- **Belonging:** Growing up as a part of a closely knit community gives kids a sense of belonging and helps them assimilate into the large culture and society. A closely-knit extended family is also a security blanket for children as they grow.

- **Value learning:** By having role models apart from their parents to learn from, children have a wider base to learn values from. They learn sharing in a group when they're amongst a wider network, they learn to behave in conformity with social norms.

- **A varied play group:** Because there is so much close-knit interaction between members of a community, the children too play together despite age differences. This makes older children become responsible for younger children who may or may not be related to them, and gives younger children role models to look up to.

- **Inculcates respect for elders:** Cultures where the grandparents have an active role in nurturing and caring for their grandchildren are more respectful of their elderly.

- **Children can't get away with bad behaviour:** Given there are so many eyes watching out for them, and ready to report back misbehaviour children do tend to be conscious of how they behave.

The bottom line: When an extended family, a neighbourhood and a community all become participatory in the rearing of the next generation, that's when we will have a nation of citizens who feel connected with each other and that, in this era of social media and personal disconnect, is invaluable. And of course, before we give our children their wings, they need to have their roots firmly embedded in the soil of their antecedents. Only then will they be able to go out into the world, unfettered.

KEY TAKEAWAYS

- Draw from traditional wisdom.
- Reach out to family to help your child grow up with a sense of rootedness. Involve immediate and extended family in his or her day-to-day—uncles, aunts, cousins, grandparents, extended family, neighbours, friends, the community at large.
- A sense of belonging at the micro-level, will create a sense of connectedness at the macro level.

STEP EIGHT: DEFINE

We all need boundaries, children more so. Children come hardwired to test how far they can go, and it is for parents to define these boundaries.

Perhaps my earliest introduction to the word 'boundary' was in connection with the crumbling wall that marked the world outside the bank quarters we then lived in. 'Don't go outside the boundary wall,' my mom would say when I was going down to play, unsupervised, of course (this was in a gentler age when kids played unsupervised and parents trusted the universe and eagle-eyed neighbours to keep them safe. Yet another example of why it takes a village, as mentioned in the previous chapter.)

As my son grew, I began creating my own boundaries for him. Physical boundaries. Behavioural boundaries. Boundaries that he pushed at every day, because that is what offspring are meant to do, to push the boundaries and then tap dance on the last standing nerve that a parent has left. As the very wise Unknown said, 'Children are a great comfort to us in our old age, and they help us reach it faster too.' Or these wiser words from American humourist, Franklin P. Jones, 'You can learn many things from children. How much patience you have, for instance.' Whether it is the toddler who keeps dumping the contents of his plate on the floor because he doesn't want the veggies or the surly teen who refuses to answer questions about school and grades, children can be rather trying when they're pushing the boundaries of what they can get away with. As Socrates said, a couple of millennia ago, 'Children today are tyrants. They contradict their parents, gobble their food, and tyrannise their teachers.' Not much seems to have changed in the current age.

And we parents are no better, at times, we push boundaries ourselves in trying to smoothen out the creases of this crumpled world for them. But boundaries we need, no matter how crumpled our worlds get, even though they might not always make us or our children happy. Dr Brene Brown states, 'I've found what makes children happy doesn't always prepare them to be courageous, engaged adults.'

Why are rules and boundaries important in the raising of a child?

Every research on the subject I've read says that rules are essential to let a child flourish, as long as they are age appropriate.

- **Rules make the child ready for the real world:** As a child grows, she will have to comply with an increasing number of rules—from playing fair in the playground, to sitting peaceably in class, to not lying. Some of these rules are applicable to larger society: being honest, resolving disputes without aggression, waiting your turn in a public situation. And all this begins at home, when they learn that the rule is 'no hitting' or that 'toys have to be picked up after playing'. When you gradually increase what you allow your child, in terms of boundaries, you also help a child increase his or her self confidence in handling situations.

- **Kids learn to behave in a social situation:** It could something as simple as insisting on 'please' and 'thank you', or not interrupting when another person is speaking, or perhaps, saying 'excuse me' if they absolutely must interrupt (something our television panellists as well as television anchors could do well to learn), and using polite language in regular conversation.

- **Rules help reduce parent-child conflict:** If there are no rules, a child never knows what is acceptable and what isn't and may not realise when he or she has overstepped the boundaries, or may deliberately push the lines. Clear rules and boundaries means no infringements are allowed and children learn that soon when they face the consequences.

- **Rules are comforting:** Kids needs rules, because they need to know subconsciously that someone else is in charge. They are too little to make so many decisions about their lives just yet, and have all the time in the world to figure things out. The rules about not touching electrical sockets, not staying up late, staying away from matches only help keep them safe. The safety and well being rules we enforce eventually help them grow up into law abiding citizens. To quote Maria Montessori, 'A child needs freedom within limits.'

Sometimes, it isn't the child who needs boundaries but the parent. At times, we ourselves blur the lines between parent and child by doing so much for them, that we completely surrender our individual autonomy. The American columnist Erma Bombeck joked that, 'When my kids become wild and unruly, I use a nice safe playpen. When they're finished, I climb out.'

A friend, let me call her A, is a very hands-on mom, to the extent she always makes me feel terribly inadequate. A high-performing corporate executive, she'd quit her job when she had her daughter and poured in all her energy into bringing up her daughter. Her daughter, a delightfully precocious and bright child, excelled through her academic career and managed to get admission into a very prestigious college abroad. A went abroad for six months, taking a home on rent off campus, to help her daughter settle in. A year later, her daughter was back home and unwilling to return to college. She couldn't cope with living on her own, and being responsible for herself. This is enmeshment, a maladjustive state of symbiosis that makes parents resentful about grown, dependent children and children dependent on parents well into adulthood.

Over-functioning as a parent on behalf of a child is often caused by anxiety. It makes us take control of things a child should be in charge of in normal circumstances. If for instance, you find yourself following up on homework submissions, packing your tween's school bag, doing their school projects for them, you're over-functioning as a parent. I'm guilty of it too, I confess, and am only just learning to gently back off, letting him flounder and bring home notes in the diary for homework not done or books not brought to class.

While it is difficult to see our kids struggle with the challenges they face, one of the greatest challenges we have as parents is to resist the temptation to rush in with our magic wands and fix it all for them. What setting clear boundaries does is provide nutrients for our children's capacities of impulse control and adaptability. These are important for a child to develop emotional resilience.

Are you crossing boundaries as a parent? If any of these sound familiar, you just might be.

- You find yourself doing things for your child, or redoing things he's done.
- You have no couple time together, your child is the focus of all your waking hours.
- You talk to your child as a peer rather than as an adult.
- You allow your child to have a say in decisions that should normally be something taken by adults of the house.
- You are completely, and unhealthily, invested in your child's successes and failures and take both rather personally as a reflection of your parenting abilities.

Take back control

Step back a little, trust in your child's ability to manage his or her achievements or lack of them, responsibilities, and disappointments instead of rushing in every single time to make things better. Know that you are doing this for his or her own good, and your child will thank you for this as an adult.

Denying a child the opportunity to experience failure and disappointment, deprives them of vital life lessons and the ability to cope with grief at various levels. Staying hands off, and letting them deal with things is what we need to do as parents, and to stay put in our roles as parents. We must draw the boundary lines firm enough and put down enough flags and markers, so that our children learn that they must keep within or risk our wrath. And when they do finally grow up enough to hit over the boundary, we will be the first to cheer for them.

To pay heed to the good doctor Benjamin Spock, 'The main source of good discipline is growing up in a loving family, being loved and learning to love in return.'

How can you set up boundaries between you and your child? Here are seven tips:

- **Spell out your expectations:** Be specific. Tell your child what you expect from them, and why you do so. 'I expect you to speak respectfully to everyone, because it is important to be polite.' 'I expect you to always tell us the truth.' 'I expect you to be responsible for your homework.' Also follow up on the expectations you've specified by not allowing any transgressions.

- **Define your values:** Let your child know what you value. For instance, honesty. Or being responsible. It makes it easier for a child to know what will be unacceptable to you.
- **Shift focus to yourself:** Instead of making it all about what your child wants, consider what you want to happen. Place your requirements in the foreground.
- **Establish consequences for a crossed boundary:** If your child keeps getting away with crossing boundaries, there will be no internal motivation to respect the boundaries set. If you want you can discuss the consequences with your child before you set the rule, so they know what to expect.
- **Be realistic about boundaries:** If you expect your toddler to eat on his own without making a mess or your pre-teen to go to sleep early every single night, you might be in for more trouble than you realise. And this sets up the ground for increased conflicts, which you really could do without. Your child might also feel that he or she can never match your standards and will probably give up trying.
- **Be consistent:** A rule is a rule is a rule, and when you stick to the rules and the consequences, the child knows what to expect if he breaks it. Instead of having too many rules that you enforce half-heartedly, choose a few important ones limited to behaviour, safety and health.

- **Limit choices:** Here's something a lot of us do because we think we are empowering our kids to learn to take decisions on their own, and facilitating autonomy. For instance, we no longer present food as a given ultimatum, but instead offer our kids options between multiple things. 'Do you want spaghetti or dal chawal?' is often heard. In the same vein, 'Do you want to go to the park or do you want to go to the mall?' and 'Do you want to wear the pink dress or do you want to wear the yellow skirt?' are not unusual either.

- In due course, a child comes to expect a choice as a given, gets flustered when there is no choice, and might get rather irate about it. Do offer choices of course, but not all the time. Interestingly, in his book *The Paradox of Choice,* Barry Schwartz theorises that giving folks too much choice makes them feel out of control and depressed. I'd think it would be like entering a huge store where you could pick absolutely anything you want, and then be paralysed by an inability to choose.

Key Takeaways

- Every child needs safe boundaries to test—whether at home or at play or online.
- Setting boundaries whether in terms of a routine, or limits in terms of behaviour gives a child a sense of security.
- And staying within preset boundaries also ingrains self-discipline and responsibility.

STEP NINE: DETACH

The child who has never fallen is the one who has been watched too much. A key element of parenting is to detach—allow kids to fall and pick themselves up again.

Perhaps the greatest favour we could do our children is to allow them to fall and allow them to fail occasionally. This is not merely about physical falls. Rather, it's about the falls and fails which will teach them lessons all our high-pitched hectoring won't.

As parents there is a natural tendency for us to want to keep our children safe from harm and protect them from the rough edges of the world, but unfortunately, this is not always a good idea, if we want them to grow up so they can navigate the world independently.

Learn from the animal kingdom

Animals learn this early, sometimes the moment they're born. Mommy giraffes go through their entire labour standing up. Think of the hapless little baby giraffe who tumbles out of the womb and crashes onto the earth from a distance of at least six feet above the ground. After this rather rough landing into the world outside the uterus, the baby giraffe must immediately gather its dazed wits and begin running around after that first crash landing if it is to survive the harsh predators of the savannah. In contrast, human infants are completely helpless when they are born and need much more intensive care by their caregivers until they are able to navigate and negotiate their immediate world. Is it any wonder then, that we tend to ... erm ... mollycoddle them silly?

Perhaps the strangest thing I saw in recent times was when I was downstairs in the building grounds keeping an eagle eye on the offspring to check if he was doing the requisite number of laps in the pool. Marching towards the changing rooms, in single file formation, were a mom, her daughter who couldn't have been more than two years old, followed by an elderly lady who was probably a grandmother and two members of their domestic staff, all bearing assorted paraphernalia. The little girl, carried by her mother, was put down gently on the ground. As the two-year-old clambered up the slide, one person climbed up behind her, another stood at the foot of the slide and the mother and grandmother were on either side. For a moment, as I looked at them, my heart ached for the little girl who didn't have the space to learn to negotiate even a small slide on her own. I was reminded of what Pamela Druckerman, the author of *Bringing Up Bebe*, wrote. She said, 'I've never seen a French mother climb a jungle gym, go down a slide with her child or sit on a seesaw ... For the most part, except when toddlers are just learning to walk, French parents park themselves on the perimeter of the playground or the sandbox and chat with one another.'

Success is usually reached via failure

Things have changed today. Parenting has become fraught with anxiety. Helicopter parenting is everywhere, and some parents don't even take their rotor blades off when they lay themselves down to sleep at night. I must confess, I've been there, done that, worn the t-shirt. This mollycoddling, done with the best and most loving intentions, has had the most disastrous effects ever. It has led to a generation of children afraid to negotiate even a playground on their own. This bulldozing of the path for our children, smoothening out all the bumps and turns for them, makes them unable to deal with the real pitfalls of life, those that will come along when we aren't with them to protect them.

Think about this. A little toddler, just about perfecting his steps, is running in a park. The ground is uneven and the child trips. Before the child can even react to falling, a parent or an adult caretaker rushes in, picks him up and begins consoling him. The child has not even had the chance to assimilate the confusion of having fallen, or registered the pain or discomfort if any and will not know that he is supposed to pick himself up after falling, deal with the pain if minor, and continue running if there is no pain. Had no one stepped in, the toddler would have perhaps been flummoxed for a moment and then, in the natural tendency of rambunctious childhood, picked himself up and run on. This toddler now will expect to be picked up every single time he trips and falls. Had he been allowed to figure out what had happened to him when he'd fallen before an adult rushed in to comfort him, he might have thought to himself, 'Oh, that was scary, but I'm okay, let me get up and get back to running.' Now, when he falls, he does not have the experience to comfort himself and deal with the situation.

We've ended up teaching our kids to fear falling, and by extension, failing—and, in doing so, we have blocked the surest path to their success. Out of love and a desire to protect our children's self-esteem, we have bulldozed every uncomfortable bump and obstacle out of their way, depriving our children of the most important lesson of childhood: that falling, and then learning to pick oneself up again are the very experiences that will teach them how to be resourceful, persistent, innovative and resilient. But, as clinical psychologist and counsellor Sonali Gupta says, 'As a parent, it is most important to be aware of how our own personal anxieties whether from childhood or adult life impact children's life.'

Controlling parental fear

Falling of course, is purely metaphorical. Falling is what we try to save our children from because we operate from a space of fear, which we then transmit to them, rather than helping our children operate from a space of wonder and curiosity. I realised this for the very first time when my son joined a new coaching class which is two road crossings away from our home. For the first few days, we dropped him to the class by car, then for the next few days we walked him to class, reiterating all the traffic safety rules we'd already taught him over the years. Then after a week or so, he had to go and return, on foot, on his own. For the first couple of days I stood at the window looking down at the busy road, huge signal, congested traffic, honking and signal-breaking cars zipping past red lights feeling my heart somersault in my chest cavity as he took a tentative step forward, then back, before moving forward again. I would then return to my perch at the window when it was time for him to return. What I didn't bargain for was the chest-swelling sense of achievement he had from the simple act of being able to negotiate the roads on his own. At his age, I was negotiating a distance of over ten kilometres through public transport and here I was agonising over two road crossings! And to add insult to injury, other mommies in the building slapped on the 'Negligent Mommy' sash and tiara on me when I told them he was going to class on his own. Then came the day when he missed his school van and felt confident enough to come home on his own by an auto-rickshaw. Alone. After I'd picked up my heart from my toes when he called me at work to inform me about this latest act of valour, I told him I was proud of him for being brave, but he needed to have called me to inform me that he was planning to take an auto because brave does not mean being foolhardy.

Making kids resourceful

Raising resourceful adults begins with the simple process of raising resourceful children. It begins when we don't help a baby to flip itself over from its back to its stomach but allow him or her to keep struggling to do it on their own. It continues when we don't hand across a toy they are reaching to grasp but keep it at a spot where they can, with a little stretching, reach out to it. It continues when we don't rush to swoop them up when they fall while they're learning to walk but allow them the moment of puzzled reconciliation that comes with falling and then learning to get back on their feet again on their own.

Aboriginal cultures in Australia considered it essential for adults to not interfere in children's activities or play. This, they believed allowed the children to tackle controlled dangers, which in turn helped decision-making as well as risk-taking abilities.

One of the ancient cultures that advocated tough love were the Spartans. A city-state in ancient Greece, boys in Sparta were taken from their parents at age seven and placed into the 'agoge' which was a state training programme designed to make them warriors and disciplined citizens. These children were housed in barracks and trained in military warfare, hunting, athletics, and yes, scholastics. When they were twelve, these boys were given just a red cloak and made to sleep outside, making their own bed from river reeds. They had to defend themselves against wild predatory animals, scavenge and steal food. Thankfully, modern life has our children live in considerably more comfortable circumstances.

In our zeal to make life comfortable for our children, we tend to step in everywhere, even in peer interactions which should be spaces where children learn to carry out their own negotiation and conflict resolution. Take for instance a play date. One child grabs a toy the other is playing with. The mother of the aggrieved child will rush in, all sirens alert and demand that the toy be returned because her child was playing with it, even though by now her child has lost interest and found something else to occupy herself. What does her child learn at the end of it all? That mamma will always step in and get her what she wants and she doesn't need to learn to protest, or voice her disapproval.

Shielding cannot be overdone

It is not always a great idea to shield our kids from ugliness or disappointment or distressing experiences. Think back to Prince Siddhartha of Kapilavastu. Born in 563 BCE to Shuddhodana, the king of Kapilavastu in Nepal, the young prince was very sheltered and not allowed to go beyond the gates of the palace. He was shielded from all visible illness, ugliness and death because an astrologer had predicted that he would renounce the world.

When Siddhartha had grown into an intelligent young man, he dared to venture out of the palace. It was then that he saw, for the very first time in his life old age, illness and death. He had never before seen such painful sights. His charioteer told him that these were inevitable in the life of every man and every person born would eventually get old, suffer from illness and die. Thus shaken, Siddhartha was full of doubts and questions about the reason and purpose of existence.

Even getting married to the beautiful Yashodhara and siring a son, Rahula, did not alleviate his restlessness.

One fine night, he slipped away, renouncing the world in the pursuit of enlightenment. While this act did eventually give us the beautiful philosophy of Buddhism, it also serves as a warning of what we might do if we protect our children too much from what we think is undesirable.

How often do we shield our children from uncomfortable news, hesitating to talk to them about terminal illnesses, death, accidents—things we think might cause them unease? We forget that children are hardy creatures, and they can deal with the truth as long as it is presented in a matter-of-fact, age-appropriate manner. In fact, by telling them the truth about most things, we give them the honour of acknowledging that we consider them capable of handling difficult news and information. Yes, there might be sadness and anxiety but that will come to them even later when they are able to process the information in a more mature way and they might even be resentful to you for not telling them the truth when you could.

Psychological immunity

There's a very important resistance we deprive our children of when we shield and protect them too much. According to Dan Kindlon, child psychologist and author of *Too Much of a Good Thing: Raising Children of Character in an Indulgent Age*, we are depriving our children of the chances to develop what he calls 'psychological immunity' when we step in every single time when we think they will experience painful feelings or hurt. Of course, I'm not speaking actual physical hurt here, where you must step up with the band aid and the first-aid kit. Kindlon's theory is that psychological immunity develops similar to the way the body develops physiological immunity. The body needs to be exposed to the pathogens in order to know how to defend itself from an attack. In the same way, kids need to be exposed to struggle, disappointment and failure to know how to deal with these situations and to develop resilience, a very important character trait for long term success.

Another clinical psychologist who wrote about this fragility of the young today, dubbing them the 'tea cup generation' because they tend to break down if they can't handle the smallest of situations, is Wendy Mogel, author of *The Blessing of a Skinned Knee*. In her book, she speaks of a generation which has had its parents be anxious on their behalf and now don't know how to deal with regular everyday stresses of life because their parents aren't around to fix things for them. Normal anxiety helps a child learn to be resilient, as I mentioned before. And a resilient child, growing up into a resilient adult can cope with whatever the world throws his way, by dusting it off, picking himself up and moving on.

Key Takeaways

- Let your child learn to fall and to pick himself or herself up—whether at play or at school.
- The resilience your child will build by learning to dealing with hurt and failure will stand him or her in good stead through adult life.
- Control your own fears to allow your kids to fall.

STEP TEN: PRAISE

Praise, like salt, in the right proportion is essential for a child's self-esteem. But overdo it and it tastes lousy.

I was always an average student. To be honest, I put no effort into studying or paying attention in class. (Psst, don't tell my son this, though). Amongst my earliest memories is of coming home one day with a stinker of a note from a rather sour-faced teacher about me jotting down long-winded stories in my school note books rather than paying attention in class. And to add insult to injury, I had even illustrated them with expansive full-page sketches of kings, queens and princesses, not to mention castles with turrets and flags. My mother took one cursory look at the note and signed it without comment.

'Let me see the story you wrote,' she said. My knees were knocking together with fear as I handed her my notebook. She read through the story without comment, and looked at the illustrations. 'That is a well-written story,' she said, with no censure or reproach. The next evening she came home with a long book. 'Anytime you feel like writing a story, whether at school or at home, write it in this book. I want to read more of your stories.'

And that was probably what set me on to a lifetime of writing. There were early stories that I would now cringe at if they were to be made public. Then came a phase of poetry so pretentious that I shudder to read them today. Eventually, I settled into writing as a profession, albeit not short stories, but instead features and reports through the decade I played at being a journalist. And now, I write books. And honestly, I think I can trace it all back to the sudden burst of confidence I got in my ability to do so in that one sentence my mother told me, 'That is a well-written story.' That confidence, I must confess though, has waned and waxed periodically over the years, but the kernel remains.

We underestimate the power of praise. We use praise stingily, like it has been rationed to us and we need to ration it out in turn. But in fact, praise can be one of the most powerful tools to mould a child and help her to tapping into her full creative potential.

Nathaniel Branden's *The Psychology of Self-Esteem* published in 1969 put forth the premise that the lack of self-esteem amongst the then current generation of American adults, was caused by a lack of praise and therefore parents were recommended using praise to boost a child's self-esteem, which in turn would impact a child's motivation and performance. In the 1960s, praise became popular because many studies showed its positive effects. But in the 1980s and 1990s, some researchers stated that indiscriminate praise could reduce motivation, create an expectation of praise regardless of effort or outcome and have a detrimental effect on self-motivation besides reducing a child's pleasure in their own achievement.

As parents, we have to be aware of not only how often we praise but also how we praise. Did you know there are two types of praise? While some praise can be helpful, others can actually have a detrimental effect. So it isn't just about telling your child, how smart he or she is, or how pretty she is, it is about using the right kind of praise at the right time.

Some cultures don't really encourage too much praise. In Eastern cultures, like the Japanese or Chinese for instance, praise is rare, but children still seem to be internally motivated. This is another extreme, a reluctance to praise that seems to motivate a child to push boundaries in order to earn praise.

Master blaster Sachin Tendulkar always yearned for a 'well done' comment from his coach, Ramakant Achrekar, but never got it. To quote Tendulkar, 'Sir till now has never told me "well-played". The reason was that Sir didn't want me to get complacent. Whenever we scored a lot of runs, we used to hope that now Sir will tell us "well-played". But it never happened. I got his call yesterday after receiving the Bharat Ratna. Sir told me "well-done". It took Tendulkar the nation's highest civilian honour to get that elusive 'well-done' from his coach.

While you might not concur on holding out on praise until your child is at the fag end of his or her career, the lesson here is simple. Praise is powerful, and praise must be earned. Sometimes we go the other extreme and not only skip on the praise but also overload on the correction. But correcting them all the time isn't really a great idea. As Bill Ayers, elementary education theorist, stated, 'Your kids require you most of all to love them for who they are, not to spend your whole time trying to correct them.'

Research has looked into what kind of praise works better than others, and has specific findings we would do well to emulate. Some kinds of generic praise might just backfire and make kids anxious about their abilities. While it might seem a great idea to keep telling your child he or she is very smart or very talented, that is not actually as great an idea as you might have thought.

So what are the two kinds of praise you should know about?

They're really simple. They're *personal praise*—which is praise for something that comes to the child naturally, like good looks or talent or intelligence and *effort praise*—which is praise for the effort put in for a task. The praise my mother gave me for that story was not for how talented I was, that would have swollen my head to pumpkin levels. Instead, what she told me, without knowing about the research I quoted above, was that the story was 'well-written.' This effort-based praise acknowledged the effort I'd put in to make the story good, and made me try harder the next time I wrote something.

Personal praise puts the focus on the talent or a quality that a child was born with. And focussing on this might make a child believe that he or she cannot improve upon what is already there. The child might not stretch his or her efforts, or take risks. Or the child might take his or her skill or talent for granted and assume it will always work in their favour. For instance, praising a child for being intelligent, rather than the effort the child puts into studying creates what Stanford researcher Carol Dweck terms a fixed mindset, in which children expect outcomes based on innate ability, regardless of effort.

Generic praise is also something you need to avoid. 'Good job' yelled out for every single thing a child does, whether mastering shoe laces or getting a B+ on his class test, diminishes the value of the praise. While we do as parents try to boost self-esteem, we also do need to not bolster up our children so much that they get an inflated sense of self-esteem for every little thing they do.

Which is why parents need to focus on praise that talks about the effort. Examples are 'I love the thought behind your essay' or 'I can see the hard work you've put in researching your science project.'

Praise the effort

With praise that focuses on the effort, you don't emphasise the outcome, which could be positive or negative. By praising the effort, you teach a child that it is important to try, to keep trying and to find a way out of millions of ways that works for him. Working towards a goal is important, perhaps more important that the goal itself and sticking to the task at hand needs to be commended. Praising effort rather than outcome, or natural ability is what will encourage your child to take more risks and go beyond his or her comfort zone. Praising how your child approaches a task, will definitely help him repeat the effort the next time he has a similar task. For instance, if your child has a sports competition, at the end of it, whether your child has won or not, make it a point to say you were happy with the fact that your child put in the effort to better his or her timing.

What constitutes praising the effort?

- **Sincerity:** Praise that a child can relate to and acknowledge and which is not over the top is praise that is good for the child. Telling the child 'I love the effect you've created with light and shade in this painting,' is miles better than saying, 'You're a genius in art.' Also, children are smarter than you think. They can sniff out insincerity and it makes them doubt their abilities because they might feel you are saying things just to make them feel better about themselves.

- **Realistic praise:** Telling your child something they've done or created is absolutely fantastic gives them no parameters by which to judge how they've improved on their previous efforts. So rather than saying 'You're a champion', when your son or daughter wins a medal in a race, you could tell them, 'You've improved on your last personal best by two seconds in just one month, and that's fabulous.' Inflating praise just raises the bar too high for the child.

- **Be specific:** 'I like how you've coordinated the colours on the slide,' is a better option than 'It's looking nice.' The downside to this though, through personal experience, is that you will be plagued by the offspring hounding you to confirm whether colours he chooses are coordinated for future power point making efforts. As Lady Bird Johnson, the former First Lady of the United States once said, 'Children are likely to live up to what you believe of them.' Telling them you believe they are improving themselves, and worth appreciating, makes them try harder.

- **Don't compare:** The worst thing you could do when you praise a child is compare him or her to peers. The comparison should always be with the child's previous self and how a child has improved, because a child's first competition should always be with himself.

- **Don't praise too often:** Too much of praise makes it expected and a blind spot to a child seeking genuine feedback. Be judicious in how often you praise a child, and use your words carefully. According to Jean Twenge, co-author of *The Narcissism Epidemic*, young adults are growing up feeling dissatisfied and lost because every single thing they do, no matter how little, is praised effusively. Getting constant positive feedback and no negative feedback makes self-esteem go through the roof but also leads to what is called narcissism, an inflated estimation of the self and a sense of entitlement.

Paradoxically, along with the rise in self-esteem, there is a parallel rise in anxiety and depression. This is because when these children are young, they are the centre of their parents' universe with their parents being at their beck and call, constantly being complimentary about their littlest achievements, telling them how special they are.

The real world, when they enter it, gives them a right shock because it makes them difficult to deal with. They are confronted with the very real possibility that they might not really be as special as their parents led them to believe, and that can be quite a shattering realisation. They need constant handholding and guidance at university and in their first jobs because they aren't used to taking the initiative. They find it difficult to deal with criticism or rejection, and being told they or their work isn't good enough after growing up with a childhood peppered with 'good tries' can be debilitating for their self-esteem. In addition to not feeling good enough, or worthy enough, these children, according to Twenge, can find it difficult to deal with being part of a team or working with others, because they've grown up believing they get a trophy just for participating.

The bottom line? Give children accurate feedback of their performance. Mollycoddling them for fear that it would impact their self-esteem just makes them more emotionally fragile as they grow. The trouble with constantly praising a kid, regardless of veracity, negates accomplishment.

Another worrying aspect of praise is that it can be manipulative. Because a child wants so much to be praised by a parent or an adult, the child will do things in order to earn that praise and not because there is any internal motivation to do the task at hand. This in turn will affect their learning of perseverance, resilience and reality checks, all traits that will stand them in good stead to navigate the real world when they grow up.

Key Takeaways

- Use praise judiciously, to encourage, motivate and reinforce your child. Children thrive on parental approval.
- Praise can be very powerful a motivator if used appropriately.
- The right kind of praise can help your child build his or her confidence, and other kinds of praise can actually work in an undesirable way to undermine a child's confidence.
- It is always better to praise the effort rather than the natural ability.
- Too much praise, as well as undeserved praise can make your child risk-averse, and decrease self-motivation.
- Praise should be sincere and specific with details to help a child improve.

STEP ELEVEN: LAUGH

What are your favourite memories of your childhood? Chances are it will, more often than not, be a moment that involved a lot of laughter.

And what are your favourite memories of your son or daughter's childhood? Most likely it will also be something that involved a fair amount of laughter.

Children also laugh a lot and look to laughter around them as a positive stimulus. Children are very amusing to be around. As Russian author Ivan Turgenev wrote in his *Diary of a Superfluous Man*, 'That's what children are for—that their parents may not be bored.' When the offspring was a baby I remember, I chortled every time he took my phone and had long gibberish conversations with voices I couldn't hear. He was a fabulous gibberish conversationalist, and paused and inflected and nodded his head energetically in these mock conversations which had us rolling on the floor, catching our sides with laughter. I wasn't quite so amused when he took my mobile phone, pretended it was a biscuit and dunked it into a mug of hot tea. But his sense of glee was so infectious that I found myself chortling despite my dismay at the ruined beyond redemption phone.

Sometimes, kids and their innocent honesty can lead to hilarious situations as my dear friend Ruchita Dar Shah, founder of First Moms Club discovered. 'My son came to me and said, Mom see I'm finally getting a moustache, do you thinking I'm hitting puberty?' She took a look and saw a faint shadow, and agreed that he probably was. 'Look mom, even you're hitting puberty,' he replied, pointing at her lip.

Over the years, the laughter has trickled down and the admonishments have taken over. Do this, do that, don't do this, don't do that. In the rush to make the child grow up, we lost out on laughter. Laughter helps release positive feel-good endorphins and is a great mood booster. The one thing you can gift your child, which costs absolutely nothing, is the gift of laughter. A child who grows up in a house that echoes with laughter has it good. And when a child has the freedom to laugh unhindered, the child is a happy child.

Making things funny can brighten a child's day, from making funny faces with a baby, putting on a silly pair of bunny ears and chasing a toddler, or even scatological jokes for a pre-teen, you have to keep changing what constitutes funny as your child grows up. Laughing together as a family is a great way to bond, also helps your child to develop a good sense of humour, something that always comes in handy for a lifetime. While we think of a sense of humour as something that comes naturally, it is actually a skill that children develop over the years and isn't actually something they are born with.

So what is a sense of humour?

A sense of humour is the ability to make things funny, and the ability to amuse oneself and others with the skill to make people laugh. Humour is what makes something funny; a sense of humour is the ability to recognise it. Someone with a well-developed sense of humour has the ability to recognize what's funny in others and can amuse them as well.

The advantages of helping kids to develop a sense of humour are many. Among them, are the ability to be spontaneous and think on their feet, to be unconventional in their take on things, to not take themselves too seriously and to be playful about life.

According to research, children who have a well-developed sense of humour have higher self-esteem, are more optimistic and have better interaction with their peers. In fact, some children might develop a sense of humour to cope with challenges like shifting to a new home, or to deal with bullies at the playground or in school. Apart from these advantages, laughing has physiological benefits as well. According to research, folks who laugh more have better immunity. To quote Oscar Wilde, one of the most acerbic wits the human race has produced, 'The best way to make children good is to make them happy.'

Different ages require differing sense of humour

As a parent you can help a child begin to develop a sense of humour from an early age. For example:

- **Babies:** While babies are still non-verbal, they are likely to respond to funny faces, or noises, and laughter, in sheer imitation. They also are highly responsive to tickling. They don't really have a context yet to realise that the unfamiliar is meant to be funny. Laughter at around four months is more likely to come from being bounced in a lap or some form of physical play. When they're between nine to fifteen months, babies understand that quacking like a duck by an adult is meant to be funny because it is against what is supposed to be regular behaviour. According to Paul E.McGhee, a development psychologist and the author of *Understanding and Promoting the Development of Children's Humour*, infants find pleasure in information they process about things that are similar to what they already know but just that wee bit different.

- **Toddlers:** With toddlers, humour is physical: a peek-a-boo, a bout of tickling, rough-and-tumble play. As kids gradually develop language at this point, they might find rhymes and actions in keeping with the rhymes funny.

- **Preschoolers:** By the time kids become preschoolers, they actually try to start making others around them laugh by doing funny things. Your child might begin clowning around the house, or do stuff repeatedly once he or she has figured out it gets you to laugh, which can be a bit of a pain sometimes. I remember a particularly trying morning where the offspring did a particular dance move gadzillion times because I'd laughed at it the first time and by repeat number 173, my face was contorted into a rictus mask of stretched muscles. Potty humour also begins around the time of potty training because this is the time that children begin getting fascinated with their body and bodily functions. With preschoolers, something that is unexpected will get a laugh, and scatological humour becomes really big at this point. Su-su potty jokes will rule, so be warned. Hopefully, they will grow out of it, but given how some adults still go hyuck-hyuck with fart jokes, some do not.

- **School kids:** School kids become more adept at joke telling, and comic timing, and often tell jokes to one another in order to make their friends laugh. They might be guilty of repeating the same joke one million times, and might mess up the punch line a bit, but with practice and some encouragement they'll get to where they're smooth about remembering it and delivering it with ease.

- **Tweens and teens:** Older kids like word play and slowly begin using sarcasm and irony amongst other forms of humour. Perhaps we, as parents, get reintroduced to fun in its purest form when we have children. As author Mignon McLaughlin says, 'Only where children gather is there any real chance of fun.'

How can you help your child develop a sense of humour?

It is pretty simple. Children learn by imitation so if you laugh and put effort into making jokes, being funny, and see the lighter side of things on a regular basis, your child will, too. Pay attention when your child is trying to be funny, laugh delightedly if it amuses you. Your child does like the reinforcement that his effort has worked. Never mind if it is really unfunny. Watch funny movies and television shows, or read funny books with your child that can help him develop a sense of what is funny and what is not. Do use your discretion though, adult humour and misogynist comic acts might not be what you want your child to emulate. Stuff that is off limits should definitely include jokes that are vulgar and offensive, or discriminatory. As also jokes that poke fun at people's disabilities. While jokes on folks who stammer or are squint-eyed are commonplace, do tell your child why it isn't really on to make fun of such people.

Why you should re-learn to laugh in order to teach your child to laugh

Most of us when we grow up stop laughing easily and naturally. We worry what folks might think of us, and whether they will find us silly. We hold back laughter, or even smiles, we put on the mantle of being grown up and some of us get so darned serious that we spend our days with an expression that mandates roughage in our diet.

And it gets more difficult to make people laugh. We turn to stand-up comics, funny television shows and books to get our laughs from because we are all too busy being serious grown ups, doing heavy weight stuff. We lose out on laughing and making folks laugh because it seems improper.

We tone down our laughter because we worry that we sound funny laughing, and gosh, our teeth aren't looking too good when we do an open-mouthed belly guffaw. But when we laugh unhindered, our children learn that it is okay to laugh and have a sense of humour, and that can make dark days brighter, and give you something to connect with your child.

Here are some ways you can help your child develop a funny bone:

- Make the home warm and supportive. It allows a child the freedom to know that he can risk being silly.
- Be as playful as you can with your child. Make funny faces, speak in accents, encourage imaginative and pretend play.
- Build your child's self-esteem enough so he or she can be funny or silly without being inhibited for fear of being judged.
- Tell stories in a humorous way. Your child will learn how to narrate amusing incidents by listening to you.
- Use humour in situations that would otherwise be tense.
- Make mistakes into jokes and laugh good naturedly about them.
- Have rules about what kind of jokes are allowed and what aren't. Put your foot down when it comes to adult humour, and don't crack adult jokes in the presence of a child, nor should you try sarcasm with a child.

KEY TAKEAWAYS

- Encourage laughter from your child. Laugh with your child.
- Teach good humouredness to your child.
- Be attentive when your child is trying to make you laugh and respond appropriately.
- Set boundaries of what is acceptable and what isn't.

STEP TWELVE: LISTEN

Listening is an art we're all forgetting, getting so consumed into the world of online communication. I know of families which can be in the same home at the same time, but will WhatsApp each other rather than sit in the same room and have a conversation face-to-face.

When the offspring was younger, we had a bedtime routine which comprised of him telling me all he did through the day and me listening. 'An den I gave A one punch, and then Miss T tole me to go to the notty corner and I sad there fer the entire period...' As you can imagine, there was much dread in anticipation of the call from school, but it gave me an insight into what had happened in his day, the time when I wasn't around.

As he's segued into a surly teen, conversations are becoming more precious and rare. So, I've changed it a bit. Instead of him telling me what he did through the day, I tell him what happened through my day. And sometimes if my day hasn't really been that eventful (after all, how much can I stretch, 'Sat down, wrote two chapters,') I tell him a story.

It could be anything, *Cinderella, The Little Prince, Ali Baba and the Forty Thieves*, a completely made-up story. It doesn't matter. As long as he listens. And asks questions. And we communicate. That, I think, is what is precious to me, the ten minutes at the end of the day, where we talk to each other undisturbed and communicate unhindered.

With children, being heard by their parents is important to them. A research project that followed roughly 800 Seattle public school children through school and into their thirties, under the programme *Raising Healthy Children*, stated that children need to be heard. The research concluded that perhaps the most overlooked parenting task these days is something that is so easy to do but often ignored, that of listening.

Extricating information from a child about his day can sometimes feel like conducting a tooth extraction with a pair of tooth picks. At times, when the offspring, now being a teen, is in one of those incommunicable moods I feel like a Spanish Inquisitor playing Twenty Questions with him. As Dr Benjamin Spock blithely said, 'There are only two things a child will share willingly; communicable diseases and its mother's age.'

As parents, we love to talk to our children. It begins from their infancy where we keep chatting to them, and by doing so help them build up the framework for vocabulary and language. As our children grow, we listen to them attentively, but often, and I'm guilty of it too, things are so busy or there is something on the fire, or something that needs to be done right now, that we hush up our kids when they come to tell us something. What does happen then, and I've seen it, is that the child eventually stops coming to tell you things. And as the child grows, he gets friends who listen to him and he takes most of his conversation to his friends or to other adults who listen.

The first thing we need to relearn as parents and by god, this was a tough one for me, is to shut up and listen. We can learn a lot from children if we just learn to listen to them. As Mark Twain said, 'The most interesting information comes from children, for they tell all they know and then stop.'

Note your body language when you are listening to something a child is telling you. Are you giving them your full attention or are you distracted by the pan on the fire, the clothes waiting to be put to dry from the washing machine, the messages pinging on your phone waiting to be answered, the presentation lurking in your laptop needing to be structured? Kids don't really look for an opportune time to tell you something. They rush in and blurt out what they have to say regardless of whether you have an ongoing conference call or the hot oil in the pan is ready to sputter up to the ceiling.

Once when I was on a conference call across multiple time zones, my son chose to clamber onto my lap, and tell me that someone at school had beaten him up that day. I could only hug him and silently gesture for him to wait until the call ended. By the time that I responded to what he had told me, he decided to clam up about it, saying he would deal with it himself the next day. No matter how much I tried to get him to talk about it again, he never did. I've always regretted that lost moment and that incomplete conversation. As a dear friend once told me, 'When my daughter comes to me with anything, I keep whatever I'm doing aside and listen. Once the moment is gone it is gone, and she might not want to share it with me again.'

When your child is talking to you, give them the gift of your entire attention, look into their eyes and listen, smile at them. Ignore the phone, the pan on the fire (of course switch it off, unless you want to smoke yourself out of the house), and as someone said wisely, 'Put on your listening ears.'

All kids are different. Some are chatty and only too eager to communicate, while others believe in grunting as an appropriate response to all questions. Getting a reticent communicator to open up can be quite a challenge but the effort will always be worth it, if you wish to stay connected to your child and know what is going on in his or her life. Here are some pointers:

Set the groundwork for conversations

Encourage your child to begin confiding in you without the fear of being judged from an early age. Put your critical hat aside, don't jump in when the child is telling you about something that happened with them, and blame them for what happened. 'What did you do for A to not be your best friend anymore?' I've been rather guilty about this myself, but I'm now learning to listen without comment.

Keep time aside for conversations

We all have busy days, not just us parents but also the children. Between school and classes and extracurricular activities, most kids have such a packed schedule that they might not be in the mind frame for any chats when they're rushing between things. I've found that bedtime is generally the best time to wrap things up for the day and have a few minutes of a leisurely conversation about anything and everything. We've discussed everything from the onset of puberty to the evolution of Justin Bieber's hairstyles and tattoos in these chats. Sometimes sitting at the dinner table makes for a good recap of the day too, where he sometimes deigns to not grunt through the entire meal in monosyllabic replies, making it more an inquisition than a conversation. Sometimes, walks to the store or to a short distance away from home also are opportunities for conversation, which are relaxed and no stress chats about anything and everything. Sometimes, the nicest conversations have happened when stuck in traffic. While I definitely don't recommend that you navigate into traffic jams in order to have a conversation with your child, but any opportunity should be grabbed with both hands.

Don't rush in to give advice

As adults, we are always edgy to jump into the discussion and tell our kids how to solve the situation or give them advice on what they should have done. This might just make your kid feel that you think he or she is not competent enough to resolve the issue by himself or herself. Eventually, your child might just come to you only when he or she needs a solution to the issue.

Let the child lead the conversation

Very often children might not want to talk about what you want to talk, and you might try to lead the conversation to what you want to talk about. This might make your child clam up and become resistant to further conversation. Instead, let the child talk about what interests them and then you could perhaps eventually take the conversation after they have chatted about what they want to talk about. Don't jump in, finish sentences, or try to put words into your child's mouth. Let them say what they have to say and then respond when they've finished, just as you would converse with an adult.

Keep the secrets

If your child tells you something in confidence, make sure you keep the secret. Telling another person, even your spouse, about what a child has confided in you could make the child lose trust in you and that is something you don't want. If it is something crucial that you must share with your spouse, make sure your spouse will not mention it to the child.

Make communication a two-way process

Sometimes the best way to draw a reticent child into a conversation could be to talk about your day, tell them about an issue you're grappling with at work, how a co-worker is shredding your last standing nerve into the paper shredder. While it does definitely make the child feel wonderful that a parent is treating him or her as an adult by this confiding, they would also learn that it is good to share and share their own problems and issues. An interesting by-product would be the occasional flashes of insights they might give which will give you a completely different perspective to the entire issue.

Use your child's name or pet name in the conversation often

American writer Dale Carnegie appropriately said that 'A person's name is to him or her the sweetest and most important sound in any language.' Our name is always nice to listen to, it makes us feel important and wanted. Children are no different. Using their name helps you get their attention when you're speaking with them.

Look at them when you speak

Look into their eyes, maintain eye contact, in a gentle non-threatening way of course. You don't want them terrified and confessing that they did in fact eat up all the chocolates despite being warned not to have more than one, when all you're doing is trying to ask them how their day went.

Make equal time

If you have more than one child, and if they're different in that one is reticent while the other is a chatterbox, it is up to you to ensure that one child does not talk for the other. Or that you don't end up giving more attention to one over the other. One-on-one conversations with your children are perhaps the strongest tools you could have to tap into a child's mind, fears, aspirations, dreams and motivations. Sometimes you might hear something that might make you uncomfortable, or challenged, or which makes you feel like an inadequate parent and that could be a trigger for change in certain unconscious behaviour patterns. As someone wiser than me said, 'If parents don't want to hear the truth, children learn not to speak it.'

My son used to train in competitive swimming. His father was in charge of taking him to the pool and bringing him back. One night, when we were chatting at bed time, my son said, 'Mom, you never come to watch me practice. Everyone's moms come.' It cut me to the quick, this statement. From that point on, I ensured I was at every practice session if I was in town and at every swim meet. The American civil rights activist Jesse Jackson rightly observed, 'Your children need your presence more than your presents.'

There's also an additional advantage in conversations with our children. It teaches them that conversation is always a quid pro quo, a two way street of listening and being listened to, a social skill that does help in the adult interaction your child would have with other adults as a grown up.

Watch your reactions

Don't lash out immediately when they tell you something you don't quite like. If something really infuriates you or you are a certified hothead, learn to count to ten, and then count to ten again before responding.

Keep your volume even

Don't get all high-pitched or yell when you're trying to get something heard. In fact, if you speak at a lower tone of voice, your children are more likely to pay attention to what you're trying to say. When you're always yelling, they tend to tune you out.

Step back

Sometimes a child might not feel like talking no matter how hard you try. In such circumstances instead of pushing it and making your child get more resentful and clam up, step back. Know you can always chat another time when your child is in the mood to chat.

Ask open-ended questions

If you want more than 'yes-no' answers, you need to make sure your questions are open ended, which make it possible for the child to say more and think about what they want to say. Respond in a way that takes the conversation further. For instance, instead of 'Did you have a good time at the picnic?', ask 'What did you like most about the picnic today?' and then follow it up with a 'Why?'

Repeat what your child says

This makes the child realise you are really paying attention to what they say, and respond with words that encourage more conversation.

And finally, be polite

Don't speak with your child in a way you wouldn't dare speak with an adult. Be respectful of a child and give him the dignity of your entire attention.

Good conversation and communication with your kids will always stand you in good stead. You will know what is going on in their lives. They will feel comfortable to come to you with anything and know you will listen calmly to them. You will get an insight into their thoughts and motivations. And that is a blessing that will help you stay connected as they grow, and hopefully through the horror of the teen years and emerge unscathed.

KEY TAKEAWAYS

- Listen to your child: To what is said and what isn't.

- Paying attention is a gift we owe our children because if we don't listen to them, they will find others who do.

- Here are some of the key points you need to keep in mind when it comes to listening to your child: keep aside time for conversations, avoid being judgmental, maintain confidentiality, make it a two-way process and always be polite.

STEP THIRTEEN: RELEASE

Good parenting is about making your child so independent that he or she doesn't need you.

As a little girl, being an only child, I spent a lot of time on my own waiting at home for my mom to come back from work. I had my books, so I never felt alone, but I was most excited to find a sparrow family had laid eggs just outside the kitchen window on the ledge. With great excitement I waited until the eggs had hatched and the little brood of baby sparrows chirped for food. Day by day they got bigger and stronger, until one morning I woke to much chirping to find the mamma sparrow pushing the little sparrows out of the nest and then swiftly moving out of the way, expecting the baby to figure out navigation and bearing the weight of its body on its own. There was agonised squawking, some awkward landings, and one which almost had my heart stop beating. But eventually the babies figured it out. And in a couple of days, the nest was deserted. The babies had flown away. The abandoned nest was eventually swept away by the maid. We humans are different. Our children, even when they leave home, can always come back, with their bagfuls of dirty laundry and be guaranteed a piping hot meal.

Animals are very prosaic about this sink or swim method of parenting. The harp seals, found in the frozen regions of the Arctic, give birth to a single pup in late February or March. The mum will take care of the baby, feeding, protecting and nurturing for just two weeks. After these two weeks the pup is left alone on the ice. The pup seals survive on their own fat reserves. For around five weeks after they're abandoned, they lose up to ten kilos of body weight before beginning to feed on crustaceans and other small fish. This style of parenting might seem a little extreme to us humans. We are so used to cosseting our offspring so much so that they come home from university with suitcases full of dirty laundry, but it gets the baby harp seals to learn survival skills quickly.

The human infant has a long period of infancy with full dependence on adults. Sometimes, well into being an adult too. We add to this by hanging on grimly to their coat tails even when our children are quite grown up, refusing to let them lead independent lives. I confess, for the longest time, I suspected I was going to be the mom tagging along like a determined spoke in the wheel on the brat's honeymoon. Wish that we could all be like the very practical Erma Bombeck, who said, 'I take a very practical view of raising children. I put a sign in each of their rooms: Checkout time is eighteen years.' I'm not even half way there yet and keenly aware of the need to keep upping the ante on making the child independent as much as possible. As American columnist Ann Landers said, 'It is not what you do for your children, but what you have taught them to do for themselves, that will make them successful human beings.' Children are born so they eventually move away from us.

Little by little, step by step, parenting is a pushing away of your child, so that by the time a child is a teen, he or she can cope with the world independently. The greatest gift you can give your child is the strength to be independent. Moving away can be attitudinal or geographical. A child can move from the parental fold even while living under the same roof, or the process may be even more complicated and painful when your child moves out of home to go to a hostel, or to another city for their first job. All those years you wished you had some quiet in the house, or some me-time, this is when you get it all, with no squalling pipsqueaks hanging onto your hems as you try to have an adult conversation with a friend on the phone. But the trouble is, that you are now so used to having all of you focused on your child you find it terribly difficult to switch back, and let them move on. Therefore, the letting go is not something that begins when kids go off to hostel or college, but is ideally a process that begins from the time your child begins stepping away from you, in tiny incremental ways. Whether it is weaning off from breastfeeding, going into day care, entering playschool, going off on their first stay over, raising a child is a continuous letting go. As Maria Montessori stated, 'Any child who is self-sufficient, who can tie his shoes, dress or undress himself, reflects in his joy and sense of achievement the image of human dignity which is derived from a sense of independence.'

Letting go is tough, not just for the kid but also for the parent. Why is it difficult for the parent, you wonder? After all, wouldn't we parents be clicking our heels and turning cartwheels at the thought of reclaiming our lives and not being at the beck and call of our little tyrants? But in truth, letting go involves loss of control and creates a void in the life of a parent who had hitherto been focussed on the child. And sometimes you might find yourself resisting it grimly. We need to know that letting go is ultimately what is good for the child, whether it is as a young child or as a young adult.

Author Erma Bombeck narrates an interesting incident about how her stepfather taught her to cycle. 'I told him not to let go, but he said it was time. I fell and Mom ran to pick me up, but he waved her off. I was so mad I showed him. I got right back on that bike and rode it myself.' That short paragraph is perhaps a metaphor for life and parenting, if ever there was one. Because it is only when we let go, that we let our child gain the courage and confidence they need to go ahead on their own.

While it is vital for a child to let go of the parental fold and step out into the world on his or her own, it is as important for parents to let go and detach themselves from their child. Probably the greatest letting go begins to happen when a child enters adolescence. The child becomes increasingly autonomous and takes his or her own decisions, regardless of your opinions. This might feel like rejection to most parents, and can be quite a bitter pill to swallow. In pre-pubescent kids, it might be a simple declaration to not want to accompany you on social visits. As they grow older, they might declare their individuation much more firmly. It is at this point that you will realise that childhood is getting over, and your child is indeed growing up.

As the kids grow older (between thirteen to fifteen) they begin preferring spending time with friends over time with parents and family. At this point, they begin sharing less with parents because they're already sharing all they can with their friends. In later adolescence, they're out of the home for most time, spending time with their friends. They're driving, dating, going out on overnight trips.

By the time our children move from eighteen to twenty-three, there is a cutting of the umbilical cord of sorts. The newly minted adults in the true sense of the term display their independence in various ways, even if we as parents need to be dragged kicking and screaming to accepting this. As parents, the role for us now shifts from managing to mentoring, a subtle shift that we must make if we are to remain on speaking terms with our offspring enough to mention them in our wills. At this point, our children will move out of home, whether to college and hostel or to another city on their first jobs. Our job now is to no longer tell what they need to do and how they should do it, but instead be around for consultation and opinion if they turn to us, without the expectation that they will do as we think they should do, but to be completely prepared for them to take their own decision even if it is contrary to our expectations. And to be wholly responsible for the consequences of that decision.

The greatest challenge at this point is to understand that letting go is not equivalent to abandoning the child but a vital step in helping a child to be independent and capable of managing on their own in the world. To recognise that children, as they grow are strong-minded individuals with their own likes and dislikes is the key to beginning to let go. To quote author Khaled Hosseini, 'Children aren't colouring books. You don't get to fill them with your favourite colours.'

I had a dose of that the other day, when the offspring had a bit of a mess up in a group project situation for Biology and I made, unasked by him, frantic calls to the other mommies of the group trying to salvage the situation. For all my efforts, I got soundly rapped on my knuckles by my own offspring. 'I will find a solution on my own,' he told me, his face set to grim, 'Don't interfere in my stuff.' I was hurt, I admit, I thought I was helping. But in fact, I had undermined his ability to manage things on his own in front of his peers, and I resolved to never do so again. It was a learning lesson for me as a parent. I had to stop micromanaging his work. It was a letting go of sorts.

Letting go is difficult. Most parents get so intermeshed with their child that they find separation, both physical and the child's phase of growing into her own, very tough to handle. Interestingly, in the US, colleges have to deal with getting parents off campus after freshman orientation. Some universities have actually hired parent bouncers, who have the rather unpleasant task of keeping hovering parents off campus. Other schools have created a new unofficial position, 'Dean of parents', to deal with parents who can't separate from their children.

We see this all around us. Parents who hand hold their children through college and then even after they're married and with children of their own. We want to feel needed and wanted, so we never really encourage our kids to be independent, instead we constantly keep stepping in to smooth things out. As a result, our children, no matter how 'grown up' they get, don't really grow up. But as Barbara Kingsolver wrote, 'Kids don't stay with you if you do it right. It's the one job where, the better you are, the more surely you won't be needed in the long run.'

When former president, A.P.J. Abdul Kalam decided to leave his village in order to pursue higher studies, his father was a source of strength. While telling APJ how he understood his need to spread his wings beyond the small town they lived in, he quoted Kahlil Gibran to his wife, who was hesitant about letting her son go away from home. The verse, and one that all parents should probably have stuck to their soft boards, goes like this.

'Your children are not your children. They are the sons and daughters of life's longing for itself. They come through you but not from you. You may give them your love but not your thoughts. For they have their own thoughts.'

To quote Dr Kalam, 'He took me and my three brothers to the mosque and recited the prayer Al Fatiha from the Holy

Quran. As he put me on the train at Rameswaram station, he said, "This island may be housing your body but not your soul. Your soul dwells in the house of tomorrow which none of us at Rameswaram can visit, not even in our dreams. May God bless you, my child!"'

There's an interesting anecdote about Swami Vivekananda. When he was to leave to go abroad for the first time, his mother offered him a platter of fruits with a knife. He cut the fruits and ate them, after which his mother requested him to kindly give her the knife. He did so, and she responded, 'So you have passed your test, and I heartily bless you for your mission to go abroad.' He was perplexed. He asked his mother, 'How did you test me, I did not understand.' His mother replied, 'When you handed me the knife, you held the sharp edge and gave me the wooden handle to hold. The person who thinks of the other's welfare rather than the self has the right to preach to the world, you have all my blessings.'

Teaching a child to grow up and think of himself in the wider context of society and letting him out into that society, trusting that he will survive and prosper is perhaps the most difficult thing for a parent to do. 'All our handling of the child will bear fruit, not only at the moment, but in the adult they are destined to become,' states Maria Montessori.

Here are some tips on how to let go:

- Know that you've done your best as a parent and now it is time to let your child go out into the world.

- Trust that you have equipped your child with enough skills, education and values to help him or her survive in the world.
- Rebuild your relationship between your child and you from one of dependency to mutual respect and understanding.
- Set boundaries to how much you step in, give your child enough space to grow.
- Set tasks for your child to master on his or her own, and the freedom to learn from the mistakes they make.
- If you feel it necessary to get help in letting go, consult a therapist.
- Fill up the void in your life when your child begins to find his or her own space, by filling your life with interests and passions that you might have kept on hold when your child was young and needed all your time and energy.

KEY TAKEAWAYS

- All the years of raising a child are geared towards the child eventually being independent enough to live on his own, and be responsible for himself without a parent's help in any way, either emotionally, mentally or financially.

- If we cling on to our children, we do them a disservice by stifling their growth.

- As they grow, they should need us less and that is in fact a compliment to our parenting skills.

- As a parent, you must maintain a balance between letting go and staying connected.

STEP FOURTEEN: PRIORITISE

You can only take care of your child if you take care of yourself first. Prioritise yourself.

So you thought we have thirteen little steps to help you raise the wonderful little bundle of contradictions you created into an adult human, and that was the end of it? Well, here is a surprise. We have fourteen steps in troth. One extra step, because, what effort is complete without going the extra mile. What is that extra step without which all these prior steps have absolutely no meaning? This is something so very simple, that you would think it was completely obvious but most of us miss it completely.

Taking care of yourself.

Very often in the rush to be the perfect parent we neglect ourselves. We put ourselves second. It becomes a default setting from the time one's child is a squalling infant and continues well into the time the child is an adult. But remember what they tell you when they demonstrate the safety instructions every time you take a flight, yes, before you put on someone else's oxygen mask on, put your own on. This applies to parenting and how.

You cannot be a good parent if you are not in a good space yourself. This means being physically, mentally and emotionally fit to parent. Parenting is exhausting, demanding and relentless. Very often, as parents we are running ourselves ragged between home, work and caring from a young child. And children can be demanding monsters at times when they're not being angelic and adorable, the latter more often than not when they're fast asleep and can be forgiven all their misdemeanours for the day.

What is self care at the end of the day? It is the simple act of putting yourself first as a human being. As a parent all our time is spent caring for a child. Some mothers of newborns confess to not having the time to run a comb through their hair in the entire day. Others have forgotten what it means to have a leisurely shower without little hands banging at the door, demanding to be let in, and for yet others even slipping into the loo for a minute comes loaded with the stress of wondering whether your child is going to do something disastrous for that one minute you're inside.

Parenting can be quite overwhelming, just keeping up with the daily to do list can be incredibly tiring. All one's focus is on the child, feeding, clothing, bathing, changing diapers, teaching, there seems to be no time left to spend on oneself. But taking time out to care for oneself is perhaps as important as caring for one's child. The most basic things we do, taking care of our own health, physically, mentally, emotionally, can only impact our parenting positively. To quote Saint Francis de Sales, 'Have patience with all things, but, first of all with yourself.'

To begin with, if you are stressed and unhealthy, you won't probably be able to parent to the best of your ability. This will also reflect in the way you interact with your child, leaving you a tad irritable and exhausted. And irritation coupled with exhaustion leads to yelling and anger, and that's not a nice place to be in when raising a child. By neglecting yourself, you are also sending out the message to your child that you don't consider yourself important, and that is not a message you want your child to get.

Even if it is one thing you do for yourself, choose to ensure you do it. It can be something as simple as taking a long leisurely bath, or finding a spot in your day to work out. To make sure you get the self care you need, you need to ask for help—your spouse, your family, friends, ask anyone who might be willing, to pitch in to watch your child while you do what you must. Science journalist Lu Hanessian has correctly observed, 'I know one thing for sure. It is impossible to find one's own balance from the outside in. I now know beyond a doubt that finding—and maintaining—our balance is an inside job.'

Very often as parents, we tend to put ourselves in second place so often that it becomes second nature. We put ourselves so much on the back burner that we end up smoked, burnt remnants of our former selves, reduced to slaves and lackeys to the imperious demands of our pint sized tyrants. In the first few months of becoming a mother, I remember being reduced to a zombie given the complete lack of sleep I was functioning on. The offspring, a tomato-faced squall with a foghorn of a yell already, slept for only two hours at a stretch and then woke screaming his little lungs out for a feed or change or whatever it was that tickled his fancy. But being a new mother, and paranoid about all things to do with childcare, I insisted on being available 24/7 even though I had enough and more support and help. It was only when I finally realised that I must grab my sleep and hand him over to my mother-in-law to care for when I was most sleep-deprived, could I become functional again. As comedian Ray Romano said, 'Everyone should have kids. They are the greatest joy in the world. But they are also terrorists. You'll realise this as soon as they are born and they start using sleep deprivation to break you.'

Making it a point to note and accommodate your own needs as a functional human being is essential if you are to parent effectively. As you take care of your child, make sure you are also taking care of yourself. There's absolutely no need to make a martyr of yourself, it will only make you increasingly resentful and you can't possibly yell at the baby for being the demanding little thing he is, that's the only way babies know how to be, unless they're being uterine contractingly adorable and gurgling.

Paying attention to yourself and your needs will be a trifle difficult when you've just had a baby, or if the baby is still young. You've attuned yourself to concentrating all your energies on the baby. Make it a point to tune in to yourself by taking little windows through the day just to do some deep breathing to relax yourself.

Think of your needs and act on them. If you are hungry, eat something. If you are tired, sit down a while. Things can wait. You need to make yourself a priority. It is alright to not have home cooked meals every single time, or to let the clothes for the laundry wait a while. The universe will not collapse. It's okay if your child goes into school one day with her uniform not perfectly ironed.

For the first seven years of my son's life, I was guilty of being completely focused on him. Unhealthily so. I had put on weight, I was constantly stressed, I was constantly weighing myself against some perfect mom idol and coming up short, I could never bake the perfect cake, or make the perfect school project and I was always missing on dress up day and scrambling last minute for costumes because I was too scattered. I knew bliss only when I gave up on trying to be the perfect mom, and thinking about myself too. As silly as it may sound, it was only when I became selfish about myself and my needs did I feel some of the stress fall off my shoulders.

I realised that along with my responsibility to my son, I'd forgotten myself. I'd forgotten that my first responsibility was to myself and to nurture myself. As my dear friend and founder publisher of FunOkPlease books Preeti Vyas, says, 'I have a chilli plant that produces the cutest, sharpest chillies. Expecting the plant to keep producing the perfect chillies without nurturing, nourishing or caring for the plant itself is unimaginable.' She continues, 'When I started practising Buddhism, I met a senior leader and began sharing the things I wanted, that I was praying for. After hearing me out patiently, she asks, "Are you praying for your own happiness?" Because you do know that all these other wishes depend on your own happiness.'

Self care can be as simple as ensuring you get enough sleep, to taking time out everyday to pursue an interest or a hobby. Or it could be consciously setting aside enough time for self improvement, pursuing it through formal courses, or even fixing self improvement goals and working towards them.

Here's what are non-negotiables in terms of self care as a parent.

Physical self care

- Eating regular, healthy meals, and not just leftovers from the kid's plate.
- Take time out for exercise, even if it is just an hour of a brisk walk around the neighbourhood.
- As much sleep as is essential and you can grab. Also when you have someone to watch over the baby, make sure you use that time to catch up on your zzzzzzs.
- Get your medical check ups done regularly. As you take your kids to the paediatrician regularly, you must remember that you too need to get your health check ups done periodically to ensure you are physically fit to handle the rambunctiousness of young children.

Emotional self care

- Allowing yourself the freedom to express your feelings, whether happy or sad. You don't always have to be in charge and in control.
- Spend time with your friends to distress on a regular basis or whenever you can find someone to babysit for you.
- Taking on only as much as you can handle.

Spiritual self care

- Meditation or prayer whatever works best for you.
- Indulging in a creative hobby that helps you de-stress.

Why should self care be a priority for every parent?

When you focus completely on caring for a child and neglect yourself, you're going to stress yourself out and this leads to a weakened immune system, and other nasties like high blood pressure, anxiety, anger issues as well as depression. This will definitely impact the way you parent positively. And at the end, this is what you want, to be: a positive, empowered parent who isn't angry and resentful, in the best health and state of mind you can be in, in order to raise your children to the best of your ability.

KEY TAKEAWAYS

- Make self care a priority.
- Take time out for physical, mental and emotional self care.
- Ask for help if you need it.
- And finally, know that if you don't take care of yourself, you will not be able to parent as effectively as you could.

In this book, I have tried to give you the thirteen core ideas towards better parenting. These were:

1. **Celebrate**: In little ways, every single day. Because your child is your own personal little miracle.
2. **Protect**: It is a dangerous world out there. You are responsible for your child's safety.
3. **Nourish**: Food for the body, food for the mind and food for the soul. Only when all aspects of the child's needs are met can a child grow to a mature human being.
4. **Love**: The unconditional love a parent gives a child is the bulwark on which a child builds its self-esteem.
5. **Inspire:** You are your child's first role model. Be one he or she can look up to.
6. **Challenge:** A child can only stretch beyond his capabilities when challenged.
7. **Connect**: Draw from traditional wisdom. Staying connected with the extended family and neighbourhood helps a child to grow up with a sense of rootedness.
8. **Define**: A child with boundaries is a child with a sense of security and ingrained responsibility.
9. **Detach:** A child who has never fallen is a child who is watched too much.

10. **Praise:** Use praise judiciously, to encourage, motivate and reinforce your child. Children thrive on parental approval.
11. **Laugh**: A child who grows up in a house that echoes with laughter is a happy child.
12. **Listen**: Paying attention is a gift we owe our children because if we don't listen to them, they will find others who do.
13. **Release**: Little by little, step by step, parenting is a pushing away of your child, so that by the time a child is a teen, he or she can cope with the world independently.

And finally,

14. **Prioritise:** Take care of yourself because unless you do, no one else will.

Sometimes it gets a tad difficult to remember all the information that's thrown at you. Here's an easy set of word clusters that could aid you in your quest.

Celebrate	Love	Define	Praise	Nourish
Challenge	Laugh	Detach	Protect	Inspire
Connect		Listen	Prioritise	Release

In Conclusion

It is a long journey raising a child from a gurgling infant to an adult, ready to step out into the big, bad world on his or her own. And not only is it damn tough work that no one warned you about when you signed up for it. But it is also immensely important work. As American writer Dave Eggers said, 'The raising of a child is the building of a cathedral. You cannot cut corners.'

Parenting is not a formula. It's a trial and error process. Sometimes you win and sometimes you lose. But remember one thing: you should be the parent today that you want your kids to remember tomorrow. The journey, so to speak, isn't just the child's. It is also ours as parents. We learn patience, responsibility, sacrifice, care, maturity. We learn how to live our lives with our hearts outside our bodies. Dr Benjamin Spock, the American paediatrician put it succinctly: 'Trust yourself. You know more than you think you do.'

We learn that no matter how much our child gets on our nerves by whining, throwing the grandparent of all tantrums in public or taking a geological era to finish a single meal, we can still look at them while they sleep and feel our hearts melt into little puddles that well up into our eyes.

There is light at the end of the parenting tunnel. It is bright and welcoming, and warm and loving, and it involves a recognition of a job well done, and a reclaiming of one's own life, after the offspring has flown the nest. When I was going through the terrible first year, when the offspring was a squawling bundle put on the planet to bleach my hair white, I could have never imagined that I would reach a day when he wouldn't be surgically attached to me. But today, I'm at a stage where he no longer needs me around constantly, and is in fact quite delighted when I'm not hovering around to check on how much he's studying or whether he's singlehandedly decimating every level on the latest game he's bought.

My role now is more of an adviser or a sounding board. We have proper conversations occasionally, we laugh at the same jokes because he's grown up and gets my humour, and at times even cracks jokes at my expense. The last, he stitched himself into a fit of laughter when he called my attempts at styling bed head hair, a crow's nest, without the crow.

I quite like what ancient cultures like the Tibetans state about the raising of a child, somewhere their philosophy resonates with me. They divide the raising of a child into four stages:

In the first five years of a child's life, the Tibetans say, the child should be treated like a king. This does not mean of course, that one obeys the child blindly, and kowtows to him. That would lead to quite an inflated ego, which might make it difficult for the child to go out into the world which would then effectively poke a pin to the bubble head, and deflate it quite suddenly. The Tibetans advocate a distinction between understanding and obeying. They don't advocate prohibiting a child from doing anything, instead state the child should be distracted into doing something else when he or she is doing something that is undesirable or dangerous. The key quality to foster in this age is the curiosity of the child. The child is yet not able to make logical choices, and punishments for mistakes will be seen as suppression by the child.

In the second period, from the age of five to ten, they say, treat a child like a slave. They advocate giving the child tasks to be completed, and to help the child through tasks he or she cannot complete with explanations and advice. The Tibetans don't advocate physical punishment at all. And rightly so. In the words of journalist Katherine Whitehorn, 'Children and zip fasteners do not respond to force … except occasionally.' The Tibetans advise allowing a child to develop a love for knowledge and to learn to predict people's reactions to what he or she does, and to work toward avoiding negativity.

The third period between ten to fifteen, the Tibetans say, is when we should begin treating a child as an equal. There is an advantage to the child being treated as an equal, even though you might know that you are definitely more knowledgeable. While it is definitely necessary to start making the child more independent, you must keep giving your child advice while being a sounding board to the child for his or her concerns. This is the age at which a child begins developing autonomy.

The fourth stage is the age of fifteen and above where the Tibetans say you should treat your child with respect. It is too late now, they say for teaching any values now, the mind has already formed and now you have to stand back and let the child be. With respect. This is no different to the great

Indian teacher Kautiliya who said, 'Treat your child like a darling for the first five years. For the next five years, scold them. By the time they turn sixteen, treat them like a friend. Your grown up children are your best friends.'

For me the journey as a parent is fascinating. I am no expert, no psychologist, no trained teacher. Like most of us, all I bring to the table is a fierce desire to do the best by my child. Yet, I realise, parenting is a dynamic process that constantly keeps evolving from year to year, as the child grows, so then must the parent. My waist though, has taken that dictum to grow most to heart, as well as the rest of me. There is no right way to parent, I've realised, and there is no wrong way. Every culture has their own distinct style of parenting, evolved over centuries and we must distil from the wisdom and research around us, as to what works best for us and for our child. But what parenting must comprise, I would say, is unconditional love, adequate discipline and boundaries, protection, nourishment, letting a child fall and finally, by letting a child go. No matter how it breaks our heart into multiple pieces.

And finally, as Oscar Wilde summed it up so succinctly, 'Children begin by loving their parents; as they grow older they judge them; sometimes they forgive them.' Hopefully, someday our children will stop judging us and forgive us. Especially mine, for all those times I told him 'because I said so.'

You may take some comfort from the dictum that 'few things are more satisfying than seeing your children have teenagers of their own.' Until that day arrives, enjoy the ride.

Acknowledgements

- Dr Manjeer Mukherjee Director—Training, Research and Development at arpan.org for her inputs on child sexual abuse awareness.
- Kavita Devgan, Nutritionist and columnist, for the inputs on nutrition.
- Sonali Gupta, Clinical Psychologist and counsellor, for her inputs on mindfulness and transferring anxiety.
- And for the delightful anecdotes and insights, all my WhatsApp mommy groups, Koral Dasgupta, Ruchita Dar Shah, Preeti Vyas and Mansi Zaveri.
- And my spouse, Kirit Manral. For being the steady rock parent to my headless chicken version.

Sources—Books

- *Teach Your Children Well: Parenting for Authentic Success* by Madeleine Levine
- *The Blessing of a Skinned Knee* by Wendy Mogel
- *Journal of Adolescent Health: The Canadian Health Behaviour in School-Aged Children* study funded by the Public Health Agency of Canada.
- *The World Until Yesterday: What Can We Learn from Traditional Societies?* by Jared Diamond
- *Bringing Up Bebe: One American Mother Discovers the Wisdom of French Parenting* by Pamela Druckerman
- *Outliers: The Story of Success* by Malcolm Gladwell
- *How Eskimos Keep Their Babies Warm : Parenting Wisdom from around the World* by Mei-Ling Hopgood

- *Baby and Child Care* by Dr Benjamin Spock
- *Genius Unmasked* by Roberta Ness
- *Mothers and Others: The Evolutionary Origins of Mutual Understanding* by Sarah Hrdy
- *The Forgotten Kin: Aunts and Uncles* by Robert Milardo

Online resources

- http://www.dailymail.co.uk/femail/article-3491585/Curtis-Stone-says-parents-let-fussy-eaters-hungry.html
- http://www.livescience.com/54605-why-are-babies-helpless.html
- http://www.theatlantic.com/magazine/archive/2011/07/how-to-land-your-kid-in-therapy/308555/
- http://www.pbs.org/parents/expert-tips-advice/2015/08/teach-child-love-learning-keys-kids-motivation/
- http://www.psychologicalscience.org/news/releases/a-fetus-can-sense-moms-psychological-state.html#.WEacc1wSfnw
- https://www.sciencedaily.com/releases/2011/11/111110142352.htm
- https://karenlebillon.com/2012/09/17/french-kids-dont-get-fat-why/
- http://www.todaysparent.com/toddler/what-to-do-when-your-picky-eater-goes-on-a-food-jag/
- http://onehandedcooks.com.au/food-jags-what-are-they-and-how-to-avoid-them/
- http://mobile.nytimes.com/2016/01/31/opinion/sunday/how-to-raise-a-creative-child-step-one-

back-off.html?_r=0&referer=http://paper.li/teachmama/1310737294?edition_id=74abfe50-9fb3-11e6-93a5-0cc47a0d164b
- https://ww2.kqed.org/mindshift/2016/07/06/how-to-raise-brilliant-children-according-to-science/
- https://www.theguardian.com/society/2014/jan/08/are-tablet-computers-bad-young-children
- http://time.com/3836428/reading-to-children-brain/
- http://healthland.time.com/2012/04/24/why-families-who-eat-together-are-healthier/
- http://www.urbanchildinstitute.org/articles/research-to-policy/practice/culturally-responsive-parenting
- http://www.babycentre.co.uk/a1040656/how-love-blossoms-between-you-and-your-child#ixzz4FP5zKA7q
- http://www.theloop.ca/theres-a-scientific-reasons-why-babies-are-so-damn-cute/
- http://psychcentral.com/news/2014/12/19/early-sensitive-caregiving-has-lasting-influence-on-childs-development/78842.html)
- http://psychcentral.com/news/2014/12/19/early-sensitive-caregiving-has-lasting-influence-on-childs-development/78842.html
- http://www.scientificamerican.com/article/infant-touch/
- http://www.scientificamerican.com/article/infant-touch/
- http://qz.com/527652/parents-let-your-kids-fail-youll-be-doing-them-a-favor/

- http://myfamilydigest.com/happy-times-how-to-laugh-with-your-kids/
- http://www.huffingtonpost.in/entry/share-a-laugh-with-your-kids_b_12715694
- http://www.ahaparenting.com/parenting-tools/connection/play-child-emotional-intelligence
- http://www.speechlanguagefeeding.com/picky-eating-problems-solutions/
- https://www.understood.org/en/friends-feelings/empowering-your-child/celebrating-successes/ways-praise-can-empower-kids-learning-issues
- https://www.globalcitizen.org/en/content/10-unique-parenting-styles-from-around-the-world/
- http://www.mindbodygreen.com/0-12268/10-eating-rules-french-children-know-but-most-americans-dont.html
- http://www.babycentre.co.uk/a1040656/how-love-blossoms-between-you-and-your-child#ixzz4FP5zKA7q
- http://www.thefamouspeople.com/sports-persons.php#2GdREBOUmvaqkd5w.99
- http://www.slate.com/articles/sports/esquire_shortgame_1/2014/12/quiz_child_prodigies_and_the_parents_who_raise_them.html
- https://www.babble.com/baby/child-rearing-around-world/
- http://www.theatlantic.com/china/archive/2013/09/in-china-its-the-grandparents-who-lean-in/280097/
- http://www.theatlantic.com/magazine/

- archive/2014/04/hey-parents-leave-those-kids-alone/358631/
- http://qz.com/527652/parents-let-your-kids-fail-youll-be-doing-them-a-favor/
- http://www.thehindu.com/news/national/telangana/adivasis-prefer-to-bring-up-their-children-the-traditional-way/article8118524.ece
- http://www.theatlantic.com/magazine/archive/2011/07/how-to-land-your-kid-in-therapy/ 308555/
- http://www.findingdutchland.com/happiest-kids-in-the-world/
- *http://qz.com/465515/how-two-orthodox-brahmins-played-a-crucial-role-in-apj-abdul-kalams-childhood/*
- https://www.care.com/a/different-parenting-styles-in-different-countries-20150312170036
- http://www.qidzaapp.com/why-its-important-for-your-child-to-laugh/
- http://kidshealth.org/en/parents/child-humor.html
- https://en.wikipedia.org/wiki/Team_Hoyt
- http://www.europeanmama.com/parenting-in-india/
- http://www.nytimes.com/2012/08/05/opinion/sunday/raising-successful-children.html?_r=0
- https://www.theguardian.com/commentisfree/2012/aug/05/phillip-hodson-parents-let-children-go
- http://www.theatlantic.com/magazine/archive/2011/07/how-to-land-your-kid-in-therapy/ 308555/
- http://fatherhood.about.com/od/activities/a/celebrating.htm
- http://www.motherearthliving.com/smart-parenting/

- kids-and-gadgets-effects-of-electronic-media-on-developing-brains
- http://kff.org/other/event/generation-m2-media-in-the-lives-of/
- http://www.parenting.com/article/why-kids-need-rules
- https://www.empoweringparents.com/article/parental-roles-how-to-set-healthy-boundaries-with-your-child/
- https://www.psychologytoday.com/blog/surviving-your-childs-adolescence/201204/parenting-adolescents-and-the-problems-letting-go
- http://cupofjo.com/2015/08/parenting-in-kenya/
- https://www.theguardian.com/lifeandstyle/2015/sep/05/parenting-tomorrow-why-should-let-children-fail
- https://www.scanva.org/support-for-parents/parent-resource-center-2/self-care-for-parents/
- http://www.ahaparenting.com/blog/Balance_Life_with_kids_self-Care
- http://www.thefamouspeople.com/profiles/wolfgang-amadeus-mozart-479.php#Ej01jRj57okAxfA3.99
- https://www.theguardian.com/uk/2006/oct/08/schools.education
- https://www.education.com/reference/article/play-creativity-problem-solving/
- https://timesofindia.indiatimes.com/entertainment/hindi/bollywood/news/Shabana-Azmi-At-19-I-prided-myself-on-the-fact-that-I-didnt-even-read-newspapers/articleshow/45979241.cms

www.ingramcontent.com/pod-product-compliance
Lightning Source LLC
LaVergne TN
LVHW010325070526
838199LV00065B/5661